SIMPLE SEASONS

Stunning Quilts and Savory Recipes

KIM DIEHL

Martingale®
& COMPANY

DEDICATION

To my parents, Sid and Patty, who helped shape my childhood holiday memories. And to my own family, Dan, Katie, and Molly, for the wonderful new memories we're building together.

Simple Seasons: Stunning Quilts and Savory Recipes
© 2007 by Kim Diehl

That Patchwork Place® is an imprint of Martingale & Company®.

Martingale & Company
20205 144th Ave. NE
Woodinville, WA 98072-8478
www.martingale-pub.com

Credits

President & CEO: Tom Wierzbicki
Publisher: Jane Hamada
Editorial Director: Mary V. Green
Managing Editor: Tina Cook
Developmental Editor: Karen Costello Soltys
Technical Editor: Laurie Baker
Copy Editor: Christine Barnes
Design Director: Stan Green
Assistant Design Director: Regina Girard
Illustrator: Laurel Strand
Cover & Text Designer: Stan Green
Photographer: Brent Kane

Printed in China
12 11 10 09 08   8 7 6 5 4

Library of Congress Cataloging-in-Publication Data
Library of Congress Control Number: 2007027365
ISBN: 978-1-56477-727-0

Mission Statement

Dedicated to providing quality products and service to inspire creativity.

CONTENTS

INTRODUCTION

DO YOU LOVE WATCHING THE SEASONS CHANGE? WITH EVERY PASSING YEAR, I FIND MYSELF ANTICIPATING AND EMBRACING EACH NEW SEASON AS IT APPROACHES. CHILLY WINTER DAYS GIVE WAY TO THE FRESH START OF SPRING, WARM SUMMER SUNSHINE COAXES OUR GARDENS INTO BLOOM, AND THEN AUTUMN'S CRISP, COOL DAYS BRING THE PROMISE OF REST AND RENEWAL AS WE PREPARE TO BEGIN AGAIN. BUT WHAT I LOVE MOST ABOUT THE SEASONS ARE THE CELEBRATIONS, HOLIDAYS, AND TRADITIONS THAT ACCOMPANY THEM. NOT JUST THE BIG THINGS, BUT THE SMALL THINGS AS WELL—THOSE LITTLE JOYS THAT ARE UNIQUE TO EACH TIME OF YEAR.

WHO CAN THINK OF SPRING without envisioning chocolate rabbits and Easter baskets, or remembering the scent of freshly cut lilacs? Can you recall barefoot summer days without thinking of the gardens you've hoed and the taste of homemade ice cream as you watched the Fourth of July fireworks? Then there are the harvest days of autumn, with spooky jack-o'-lanterns and warm, spicy aromas wafting from the kitchen. Finally, winter brings the hustle and bustle of the holiday season, with children's mitten-clad fingers building snowmen and the twinkle of lights among the mistletoe and holly. The quilts shared in this book help bring these special moments to life and celebrate the memories that live within us.

As you glance through the photographs that follow, notice how these quilts set the mood for each room and unify the decorating themes of each season. Holiday quilts are a wonderful way to mark a special day, but with an imaginative approach to color, I believe seasonal quilts can impart the spirit of celebration long before and after the actual event itself. And quilts aren't just for beds! Display them on tabletops, spill them from crocks and baskets, and drape them over chairs and sofas. Your family will reach for them again and again as they experience the memorable moments each season brings.

And when it comes to living and celebrating the seasons, what could be better than special meals or dishes made from your favorite recipes? So many quilters I meet are wonderful cooks, perhaps because quilting and cooking seem to go hand in hand. Both pastimes are a treat for the senses, and both reflect the sensibilities and personal flair of the maker.

As my children have grown and our family has established its own traditions, shared meals have played an important role in our lives. I have fond memories of my mother and grandmother emerging from the kitchen with rosy cheeks and special dishes that were uniquely theirs—some were served only during a particular season or holiday, and I looked forward to them so much. Times have changed, and now I'm the cook with rosy cheeks, but my daughters are no different. As we enter each new season of the year, favorite family dishes are greatly anticipated and often requested. I'm happy to share some of these recipes with you, and I hope that your family will enjoy them as well.

I wish you many seasons of wonderful memories. By lending those special touches that only we can bring, we enrich the lives of our families today and help build their memories for tomorrow.

FABRIC SELECTION

WHEN I SELECT MY FABRICS, I CHOOSE ONLY HIGH-QUALITY, 100%-COTTON CLOTH. I BELIEVE THAT MY FABRIC CHOICES, EVEN MORE THAN THE BLOCK PATTERNS AND DESIGNS, SET THE TONE IN EACH QUILT. TO SIMPLIFY THE PROCESS AS I AUDITION MY FABRICS, I USE THE FOLLOWING GUIDELINES:

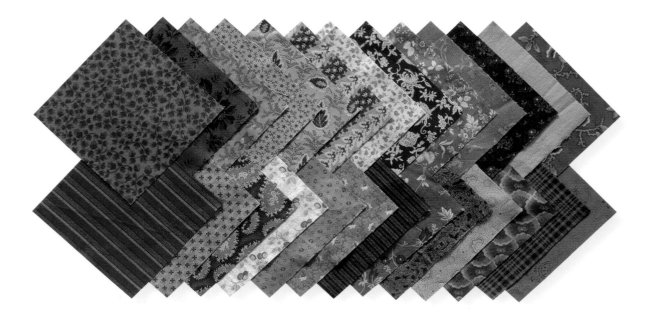

- For a more traditional or formal look, I choose fewer colors and repeat them throughout the quilt top. As a general rule, I use just one print for each color.
- For a bit of the make-do look, I select the prints for my main color scheme, and then add several look-alikes to imply that I ran short of my original selection and had to substitute others. This method ensures success when there are several perfect prints to choose from.
- To achieve a planned scrappy look, I select colors and prints as I would for a make-do quilt, and then add several lighter, brighter, and darker shades, along with a few complementary colors. I vary the scale of the prints for interest, but I also make sure my choices work well together and appear deliberate.

- For a completely scrappy look, I take the previous guidelines a step further by including colors and prints that are slightly off, but not glaringly so. Experience has taught me that it's easy to incorporate a wide variety of prints simply by deciding at the start whether my colors will be muted and muddy or clear and bright.
- My favorite method for auditioning fabrics is to toss them in a pile on the floor, and then step back to evaluate them from a short distance. If one fabric consistently acts as a bull's-eye, regardless of how it's placed in relation to the others, I remove it from the mix.

I hope these guidelines will be helpful as you make your fabric choices, but remember that first and foremost, you should listen to your instincts and please yourself.

QUILTMAKING PRINCIPLES

REFER TO THIS SECTION FOR TECHNIQUES AND PROCEDURES USED TO PIECE AND ASSEMBLE THE PROJECTS FEATURED IN THIS BOOK. SOME OF THESE TIME-HONORED PROCEDURES ARE COMMONLY PRACTICED BY QUILTMAKERS, WHILE OTHERS ARE MY OWN METHODS, LEARNED THROUGH THE TRIALS AND ERRORS OF SELF-TEACHING. I ENCOURAGE YOU TO READ THESE TECHNIQUES CAREFULLY AND TO INCORPORATE THEM INTO YOUR OWN QUILTMAKING ROUTINES.

Yardage Requirements

The project instructions in this book assume a 42" useable width of fabric after prewashing and removing selvages. To make the best use of your yardage, always cut the pieces in the order given.

Rotary Cutting

Unless otherwise instructed, cut all pieces on the straight of grain and across the width of the fabric. To speed the cutting process, I fold my pressed fabric in half with the selvages together, and then in half once more. This method results in four pieces with each cut. Of course, the size of the pieces will determine how many folds you can make.

Place the folded fabric on your cutting mat, aligning the folded edge with a horizontal line on the marked grid. Position your ruler on top of the fabric and make a vertical cut along one side to establish a straight edge. Measure and cut your pieces from this edge.

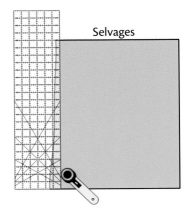

Selvages

To cut half-square triangles from a square (or layered stack of squares), lay your ruler diagonally across the square, with the cutting edge directly over the corners, and make the cut.

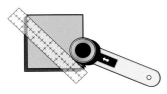

Pinning

I recommend pinning your layered patchwork pieces together at regular intervals, including all sewn seams and intersections. A good tip for sewing a consistently straight seam to the back edge of your patchwork is to pin the pieces with glass-head pins. The pin heads can be used to steer the patchwork through the machine in a straight line, eliminating inaccurate seams at the tail end where fishtailing often occurs.

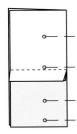

Machine Piecing

Unless otherwise instructed, join your fabrics with right sides together using a ¼" seam allowance. To achieve an accurate seam allowance, use a ¼" presser foot made specifically for quiltmaking. You can also make a guide using masking tape. Simply lower your sewing machine needle until the point rests upon the ¼" line of an acrylic ruler. After ensuring that the ruler is resting in a straight position, apply a line of ¼" masking tape to the sewing machine surface exactly along the ruler's edge, taking care not to cover the feed dogs. Align the edge of the fabrics with this taped line as you feed the pieces through the machine.

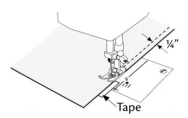

Your machine's standard stitch length will be fine for most projects. However, for smaller-scale patchwork pieces, I recommend reducing your stitch length slightly to achieve a secure seam to the very edges of your joined pieces.

Strip Piecing

Several projects in this book call for strips of fabric to be sewn into sets, which are then cut into measured segments. I recommend pressing the seam allowance of each new strip as it is added, referring to the pattern instructions. After the strip set is pressed, position it squarely on the cutting mat. Align a horizontal line on your ruler with a seam line and cut through the strip set at one end to establish a straight edge. Measure and cut your segments from this edge.

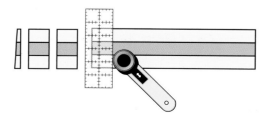

Chain Piecing

For projects with many pieces to be joined, chain piecing saves both time and thread. To chain piece, simply feed your patchwork units through the sewing machine one after another without snipping the threads between each. When you finish sewing, cut the threads connecting the units and press as instructed.

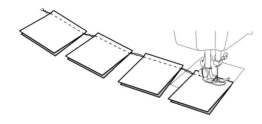

Pressing Seams

Pressing well is crucial for patchwork that fits together properly. The following steps outline my pressing method:

1. Place the patchwork on a firm-surfaced ironing board, with the fabric you wish to press toward (usually the darker fabric) on top. On the wrong side of the fabric, briefly bring a hot, dry iron down onto the sewn seam to warm the fabric.

2. Lift the iron and fold the top piece of fabric back to expose the right sides of the fabrics. While the fabric is still warm, run your fingernail along the sewn thread line to relax the fibers at the fold.

3. Press the seam flat from the right side of the patchwork. The seam allowance will lie under the fabric that was originally positioned on top.

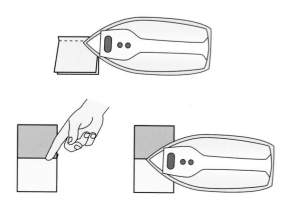

Pressing Triangle Units

Several projects in this book call for stitch-and-fold triangle units that are created by layering a square with a drawn diagonal line on top of a second square or rectangle. After stitching the pair on the line, I recommend the following steps:

1. Fold the top triangle back and align its corner with the corner of the bottom piece of fabric to keep it square; press in place.

2. Trim away the excess layers of fabric beneath the top triangle, leaving a ¼" seam allowance.

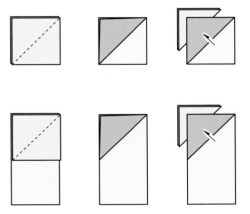

The seam allowances of triangle units are commonly trimmed *before* they are pressed, but I've found that the method above produces accurate patchwork that seldom requires squaring up.

Appliqué Methods

If you admire appliqué quilts but are hesitant to make them, I encourage you to try my machine- or hand-appliqué method. With a little practice, you'll easily master these techniques.

Invisible Machine Appliqué

This timesaving technique will enable you to use your sewing machine to achieve truly invisible stitches.

In addition to standard quilting supplies, you'll need the following tools and products for my invisible machine appliqué method:

- .004 monofilament thread in clear and smoke colors
- Bias bars of various widths
- Embroidery scissors with fine, sharp points
- Liquid fabric basting glue (water-soluble and acid-free)
- Fabric glue stick (water-soluble and acid-free)
- Freezer paper
- Iron with a sharp pressing point
- Open-toe presser foot
- Sewing machine with adjustable tension control and capable of producing a tiny zigzag stitch
- Size 75/11 machine quilting needles
- Tweezers with rounded tips

Preparing Pattern Templates

When a project features multiple appliqués made from any one pattern, I make a cardboard-weight template to trace around the shape for the required number of paper pattern pieces, rather than tracing *over* the pattern sheet numerous times. As you prepare your templates, keep in mind that any shape can be modified to fit your skill level. Simply fatten thin points and plump narrow inner curves.

1. Use a pencil to trace the pattern onto the paper (nonwaxy) side of a piece of freezer paper. With waxy sides together, pin a second piece of freezer paper under the drawn pattern.

2. Cut out the shape exactly on the drawn line and touch it with the tip of a dry, hot iron to anchor the pieces together. Remove the pin and finish fusing the pieces.

Preparing Paper Pattern Pieces

Always cut paper pattern pieces exactly on the drawn lines; you'll add the seam allowances later as you cut the shapes from fabric. To achieve smooth pattern edges, move the paper, rather than the scissors, as you take long cutting strokes.

Use the prepared template (or pattern sheet, if you are preparing just a few pieces) to trace the specified number of pattern pieces onto the paper side of a piece of freezer paper. To save time when many pieces are required, stack the freezer paper four to six pieces deep, pin the layers, and cut several at once.

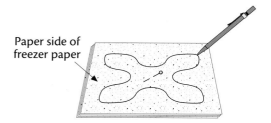

Paper side of freezer paper

Prepare mirror-image pieces by tracing the pattern onto one end of a strip of freezer paper, and then folding it accordion style. Pin the layers together and cut out the shape. When you separate the pieces, every other shape will be a mirror image.

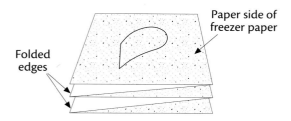

Folded edges

Paper side of freezer paper

Preparing Appliqués

1. Apply a small amount of glue from the fabric glue stick to the paper side of each pattern piece and affix it to the wrong side of your fabric, leaving approximately ½" between each shape for seam allowances. Position the longest lines or curves on the diagonal, because bias edges are

easier to manipulate than straight-grain edges when pressing the seam allowances over the paper shapes.

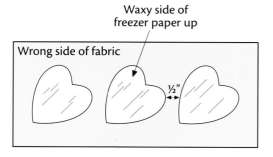

Waxy side of freezer paper up

Wrong side of fabric

½"

2. Using embroidery scissors, cut out each shape, adding a scant ¼" seam allowance around the paper. Clip the seam allowance of all curves, stopping two or three threads away from the paper edge (this will preserve an intact fabric edge when the seam allowance is pressed onto the waxy side of the pattern piece). Outer seam-allowance points do not require clipping, so an unclipped area of approximately ½" on each side of a point is fine. Small, pronounced curves need more clips to ease the seam allowance around the paper shape, while gently flowing curves require fewer clips. Clip inner points, such as the one at the top of a heart shape, up to the paper edge, taking care not to clip into the paper.

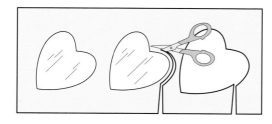

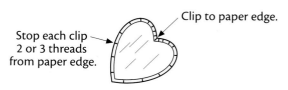

Stop each clip 2 or 3 threads from paper edge.

Clip to paper edge.

Pressing Appliqués

Shapes that are pressed well are easy to work with, resulting in finished appliqués that appear hand stitched. Use the steps that follow to press the seam allowance of each appliqué, keeping the edge you are working with furthest from you at the twelve o'clock position. If you are right handed, move the iron from right to left as you press, rotating the appliqué clockwise in small increments to keep the area you are pressing at the top of the shape. If you are left handed, simply reverse your directions as you press and rotate the appliqué.

1. Use the point of a hot, dry iron to press the seam allowance over onto the waxy side of the pattern piece, beginning at a straight or gently curved edge and working your way around the entire shape. Always direct the seam allowance toward the center of the shape because puckers or pleats can form along the appliqué edge if the seam allowance lies at an angle. Use the point of an awl or a seam ripper to help you grab and manipulate the fabric on smaller shapes.

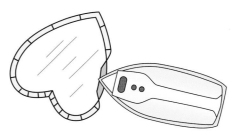

Direct seam allowance
toward center of shape.

2. For sharp outer points, press the seam allowance so the folded edge of the fabric extends beyond the first side of the pattern point. Fold over the seam allowance on the remaining side of the point and continue pressing. Apply a small amount of gluestick to the inside fold of fabric at the point. Use the point of an awl or seam ripper to drag the fabric fold in and away from the appliqué edge, and touch it with the point of a hot iron to fuse it in place.

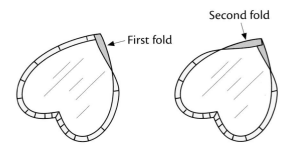

First fold · Second fold

3. To prepare a sharp inner point, use a sweeping motion to press the seam allowance leading up to the point onto the waxy side of the pattern piece. Pull the seam allowance on the remaining side of the point over onto the waxed paper and follow with the point of the iron.

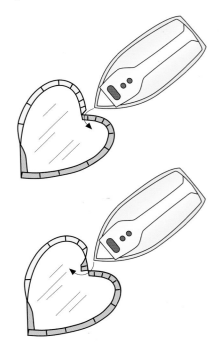

Always turn your prepared appliqué over to evaluate your pressing. From the back, loosen any pressed edges that aren't smooth, and re-press. Tiny imperfections don't require re-pressing and can usually be nudged into place with the point of your iron.

Making Bias-Tube Stems and Vines

For easy stems and vines that don't require the seam allowances to be turned under, I use bias tubes. Cut the fabric strips as specified in the project instructions and prepare them as follows:

1. With *wrong* sides together, fold the strip in half lengthwise and stitch a *scant* ¼" from the long raw edges to form a tube. For narrow stems, trim the seam allowance to ⅛" so that it will not be visible from the front.

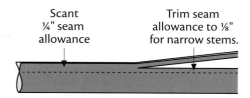

Scant ¼" seam allowance

Trim seam allowance to ⅛" for narrow stems.

2. Insert a bias bar into the tube and slide it along as you press the stem flat, centering the seam allowance so it will be hidden when you turn the stem to the front.

Bias bar

3. Place tiny dots of liquid basting glue at approximately 1" intervals under the bottom layer of the seam allowance and use a hot iron to fuse it in place.

These preparation steps will produce stems that are easy to work with. You'll notice as you lay out your stems that they often include a little extra length for flexibility. Once you're satisfied with their placement, trim away any unnecessary length.

Basting Appliqués

Invisible machine appliqué, like hand appliqué, is sewn in layers from the bottom to the top. Before you begin stitching, lay out the prepared appliqués on the background to ensure that everything fits and is to your liking. Remove all but the bottom appliqués and baste them in place using pins (taking care not to place them in the path of your stitching) *or* with liquid basting glue. Liquid basting glue is my preferred method because there are no pins to stitch around or remove and the appliqués do not shift as they are stitched.

To glue-baste an appliqué, anchor it to the background using a single pin at the center of the shape. Fold one half back to expose the pressed fabric seam allowance and place tiny dots of liquid glue onto the fabric at approximately 1" intervals; unfold and press firmly back in place. Repeat with the remaining half of the appliqué and remove the pin.

Preparing Your Sewing Machine

For invisible stitches, monofilament thread is used to stitch the appliqués in place. When selecting your monofilament color, match it to the appliqué, not the background. Generally, smoke thread is best for medium and dark prints, and clear thread for bright or pastel hues. If the spool pin on your machine will allow the monofilament thread to stand upright, choose this position because it will help regulate the tension as the thread feeds through the needle.

1. Use a size 75/11 quilting needle in your sewing machine and thread it with monofilament.

2. Wind the bobbin with standard neutral-colored thread or thread to match your background.

3. Program your sewing machine to the zigzag stitch, adjust the width and length to achieve a tiny stitch as shown below, and reduce the tension setting. For many sewing machines, a width, length, and tension setting of 1 produces the perfect stitch.

Approximate stitch size

Stitching the Appliqués

Before stitching your first project, I recommend experimenting with a simple pattern from your project to become comfortable with this technique and to find the best settings for your sewing machine.

1. Slide the basted appliqué under the sewing machine needle from front to back to direct the threads behind the machine and prevent thread snarls.

2. Position the background so the needle will pierce the fabric next to the appliqué when it is lowered. Place your fingertip over the monofilament tail and hold it while the machine takes two or three locking stitches. If your machine does not offer a locking-stitch feature, reduce the stitch length to the shortest setting and take two or three small stitches in place, *or* ensure that your starting stitches are overlapped by approximately 1" as you finish your stitching.

   Note: The placement of the first zigzag stitch may vary depending on your machine. If your model is designed to drop the first stitch inside the appliqué, position your background accordingly.

3. Lift your fingertip from the monofilament and begin zigzag stitching so that the inner stitches land a couple of threads inside the appliqué, and the outer stitches drop into the background fabric exactly next to the appliqué. I recommend watching the outer stitches while you sew to keep them positioned correctly, and the inner stitches will naturally fall into place. After stitching a short distance, pause and carefully clip the monofilament tail close to the background.

   Note: If dots of bobbin thread show on the front of your appliqué as you stitch, further adjust the settings on your machine (usually the tension control) until they disappear.

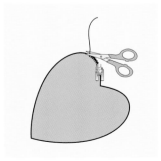

Stitch curved appliqués at a slow to moderate speed to maintain control as you steer the shape under the needle. Gently swivel the background as you stitch, stopping and pivoting as often as needed to keep the edge of the appliqué feeding straight toward the needle.

4. To firmly secure an inner point, stitch to the position where the inner stitch rests exactly on the inner point of the appliqué, and stop. Pivot the fabric so the appliqué inner point is at a right angle to the needle, and the next stitch will pierce the background. You may wish to pivot and stitch twice to secure this delicate area. After ensuring the appliqué edge is properly aligned under the presser foot, continue stitching.

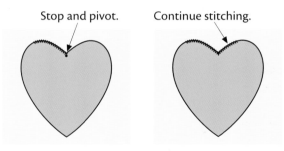

Stop and pivot.   Continue stitching.

5. To secure an outer point, stitch to the position where the outer stitch lands exactly outside the appliqué point and pierces the background, and stop. Pivot the background so the unsewn edge of the appliqué is aligned to feed under the presser foot. As you begin sewing again, a second stitch will drop into the point of the appliqué, often into your last stitch.

Stop and pivot.   Continue stitching.

6. Continue stitching around the perimeter of the appliqué until you overlap your starting point by approximately ½". End with a locking stitch

or take two or three straight stitches in place. Carefully clip the thread tails.

Note: You can place your locking stitches within the appliqué or in the background. I position my starting and stopping points where the fabric's print will disguise them best.

String Appliqué

When two or more appliqués are in close proximity on the same layer, I recommend using my string appliqué method to speed the sewing process and save thread.

1. Stitch your first appliqué as instructed in "Stitching the Appliqués" on page 12, but instead of clipping the threads when you finish, lift the presser foot and slide the background to the next appliqué without lifting it from the sewing machine surface. Lower the presser foot and resume stitching, remembering to begin and end with a locking stitch.

2. Remove the background fabric from the sewing machine after the cluster of appliqués has been stitched and carefully clip the threads between each.

Removing Paper Pattern Pieces

1. On the wrong side of the appliqué unit, use embroidery scissors to carefully pinch and cut through the fabric at least ¼" inside the appliqué seam, taking care not to puncture the freezer paper. Trim away the background fabric, leaving a generous ¼" seam allowance.

2. Grasp the appliqué between the thumb and forefinger of one hand and the appliqué seam allowance with the thumb and forefinger of your other hand; give a gentle but firm tug to free the edge of the paper pattern piece. Use the tip of your finger to loosen the glue where the pattern piece is anchored to the fabric. Peel away and discard the paper. If any paper remains in the appliqué corners, use a pair of tweezers to carefully remove it. It isn't necessary to remove any bits of paper that are too tiny to see or grasp easily.

Note: Do not cut away the background of any appliqué that doesn't contain paper, such as a stem.

Completing the Machine-Appliqué Process

Working from the bottom layer to the top, continue basting and stitching appliqués until each one has been stitched in place. As you stitch the appliqués, keep in mind that it's not necessary to stitch any edge that will be overlapped by another appliqué. If necessary, lay the completed work face down on your ironing board and lightly press from the wrong side. Take care not to apply prolonged or high heat to the appliqués, particularly from the front, because this can weaken the monofilament threads.

Turn-Free Hand Appliqué

If you love hand sewing or just like the option of on-the-go needlework, the following techniques will help you prepare portable projects.

In addition to the items outlined in "Invisible Machine Appliqué" on page 9, you'll need these supplies:

- Fine-gauge thread in a variety of colors
- Straw appliqué needles (size 9 or 10 needles work well for me)
- Thimble

Preparing and Stitching the Appliqués

1. Prepare the appliqués as outlined in "Invisible Machine Appliqué."

2. After laying out the prepared appliqués on the background, remove all but the bottom appliqués and baste them in place as instructed in "Basting Appliqués" on page 12.

3. Cut a length of thread in a color to match the appliqué and insert one end through the eye of the needle. To tie a knot, form a small loop near the tail end of the thread, rolling it between your thumb and forefinger two or three times to draw the end through the opening. Pull the loop tight to form a knot.

4. Bring the needle up from the wrong side of the background, just inside the appliqué, catching two or three threads along the appliqué edge. Pull the thread until the knot is flush with the fabric.

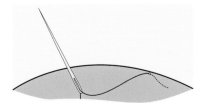

5. Insert the needle into the background just behind the point where the thread exits the fabric and come back up through the appliqué a tiny distance in front of your last stitch, again just catching the threads along the appliqué edge. Gently pull the thread until the stitch is secure. Continue stitching around the appliqué in this manner, taking tiny stitches to secure it firmly to the background. Sewing small, sturdy stitches will ensure that the appliqué remains secure when you remove the paper pattern piece.

Note: As you come to a point or corner in an appliqué shape, take two stitches to fasten the edge securely to the background.

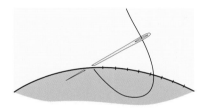

6. When you return to your starting point, insert the needle and bring it out on the wrong side of the background. Take two or three small backstitches just inside the appliqué edge, drawing the thread through the loop each time to secure it and keep it well hidden under the appliqué. (Threads that are tied off under the background fabric can create a shadow effect through fine or light-hued fabrics.) Carefully clip the thread tail.

7. Referring to "Removing Paper Pattern Pieces" on page 14, carefully remove the freezer paper.

Completing the Hand Appliqué Process

Remember to work from the bottom layer to the top when stitching your appliqués and don't forget to remove the paper pattern pieces before each new layer is added. If necessary, lay the completed piece face down onto a towel and lightly press it from the wrong side.

Embellishments

Details are often what set one quilt apart from another. Sometimes all it takes is a touch of embroidery or a lightly stuffed appliqué to make the difference.

Embroidery

The embroidery accents featured in this book were stitched using a size 5 embroidery needle and #8 perle cotton *or* two strands of embroidery floss. Perle cotton results in a slightly heavier line, while floss produces finer lines and a more subtle finish—the choice is yours. Use an embroidery hoop if desired.

French Knots

Insert your needle containing knotted thread through the background from the back, pulling until the knotted end is flush with the fabric. Wrap the thread around the needle three times while holding it near the fabric surface. Insert the needle back into the fabric a few threads away. Holding the thread leading up to the wraps slightly taut, pull the needle and trailing thread through the fabric slowly and smoothly. Tie off the thread on the back after making the desired number of French knots.

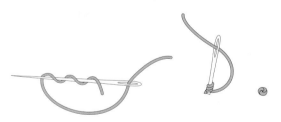

French knot

Stem Stitch

Prepare and insert your threaded needle from the back of the fabric as instructed for "French Knots." Working from the front, insert the needle into the background about ¼" behind the point where the thread first comes up through the fabric, and bring it up again at the midpoint of the stitch. Gently pull the thread taut so it lies flush with the fabric.

Continue making even stitches in this manner, pulling each stitch with equal tautness to form a sewn line of thread. Tie off the thread from the back after you complete the stitching.

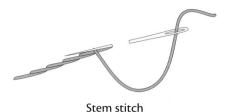

Stem stitch

Stuffed Appliqués

A simple but effective way to accent your appliqués is to stuff them with a layer of thin batting. For best results, I recommend stuffing single-layer appliqués (such as leaves or stars) or the top-most shape *only* on motifs that have multiple layers (such as the center of a flower).

1. Referring to "Preparing Pattern Templates" on page 9, use a pattern template corresponding to the appliqué you wish to stuff to trace the shape onto thin cotton batting (a water-soluble marker works best for this step).

2. Cut the shape from the batting just inside the drawn lines.

3. After the background fabric has been trimmed from the appliqué and the paper pattern piece has been removed as instructed in "Removing Paper Pattern Pieces" on page 14, insert the batting from the back of the appliqué. Use the point of an awl or a seam ripper to tuck the batting under the appliqué seam allowance so it lies smooth and flat.

4. Apply tiny drops of liquid basting glue to the batting beneath the seam allowance, using just a few drops around the perimeter. Briefly touch the stuffed appliqué from the back with a hot iron to heat-set the glue and anchor the batting.

Completing the Quilt Top

Once your blocks or units are completed, assembling them and adding borders is the next step. Here are some things to remember as you get closer to completing your quilt.

Assembling the Quilt Center

I recommend using a design wall or a large area of floor space to lay out your blocks and evaluate the balance of color. To define and visually anchor the quilt center, position blocks or units with strong hues in the corners.

For greater ease when assembling large tops, join the rows in groups of two or three. Next, join the grouped rows, working from opposite ends toward the middle, until you join the two halves.

Adding Borders

Patchwork borders contain numerous pieces or pieced units that are joined to achieve a designated length, while whole-cloth borders are cut from one length of fabric. All of the border measurements in this book are mathematically correct, but because there is little or no stretch to whole-cloth borders cut from the lengthwise grain, you may wish to slightly increase the designated lengths for greater ease when pinning and sewing. Any excess length can be trimmed after the borders are added.

When joining border strips to the center of a quilt, fold each border piece in half to find the midpoint, and then finger-press a crease. Next, fold each side of the quilt center and crease the midpoint position. Line up the creases and pin for a perfect fit.

Finishing Techniques

There are many choices available for finishing your quilt, and your decisions will enable you to tailor the appearance of your project to suit your individual preferences.

Batting

For a contemporary look, polyester batting has minimal shrinkage after washing and is a good choice when paired with prewashed fabrics. If you prefer a softly puckered, old-fashioned look, try combining thin cotton batting with fabrics that haven't been prewashed. Always follow the manufacturer's instructions for the batting you choose.

Backing

I cut and piece my quilt backings to be 3" to 4" larger than the quilt top on all sides. When you choose your backing fabric, remember that busy prints will make your quilting less visible, while muted prints and solids will emphasize your quilting design. To prevent shadowing, use fabrics in colors similar to those in your quilt top.

For the best use of yardage, seam your quilt backings as follows:

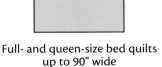

Lap quilts
up to 74" square

Twin-size bed quilts
up to 74" wide

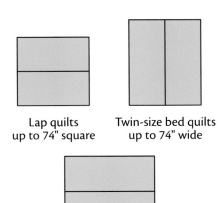

Full- and queen-size bed quilts
up to 90" wide

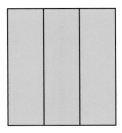

King-size bed quilts
up to 107" wide

Basting

To prepare your finished top for the quilting process:

1. Place the backing fabric, wrong side up, on a large, flat surface. Smooth any wrinkles and secure the edges with masking tape.

2. Center the batting on the backing fabric and smooth any wrinkles.

3. Carefully center the quilt top on the layered batting and backing.
   - For hand quilting, baste from corner to corner using white thread (colored thread can leave tinted fibers). Next, baste vertically and horizontally at 3" to 4" intervals.
   - For machine quilting, place size 2 rustproof safety pins 4" to 5" apart, beginning in the center and working toward the edges.

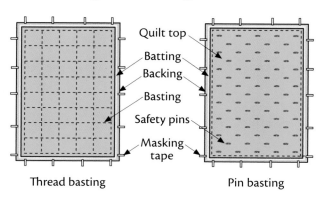

Quilt top
Batting
Backing
Basting
Safety pins
Masking tape

Thread basting   Pin basting

Marking Quilting Designs

If you plan to outline existing shapes or stitch in the ditch (along the seam line), it may not be necessary to mark your quilting design. You can use various widths of masking tape as a guide for stitching straight lines or background grids, but remember to remove the tape at the end of each day to prevent adhesive residue from damaging the fabric. More elaborate designs should be marked onto the top before you assemble the layers using a quilter's silver pencil or a fine-tipped water-soluble marker. To ensure the lines can be removed, always test your water-soluble marker on a fabric swatch before marking your top.

Whether you choose to hand or machine quilt, ensure that your project includes an adequate amount of quilting. Beautiful quilting can elevate the status of even the simplest quilt, while the most striking quilt will suffer in appearance if the quilting is scant.

Quilting

Quilting stitches are more than simply the glue that holds the layers together; they're the crowning touch on your project. Choose your favorite method or even try different methods in combination to add a final design element.

Hand Quilting

To hand quilt your project, place the quilt in a hoop or a frame and follow these steps:

1. Tie a knot in the end of a length of quilting thread approximately 18" long and insert the needle into the quilt top approximately 1" from where you wish to begin quilting.

2. Slide your needle through the layers and bring it up through the quilt top, gently tugging until the knot pops into the batting between the layers of fabric.

3. Make small, even stitches, taking care to stitch through all layers.

4. As you near the end of the thread, make a knot about ⅛" from the quilt top and insert the needle, sliding it through the batting only. Bring the needle up through the top about 1" beyond your last stitch, tugging gently until the knot disappears; carefully clip the thread.

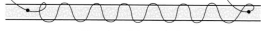

Hand-quilting stitch

Big-Stitch Quilting

The big-stitch style of hand quilting is one of my favorites. A stitch length of ⅛" to ¼" is perfectly acceptable, making it a quick and satisfying technique. Use a size 5 embroidery needle with #8 perle cotton to sew a running stitch through the layers, beginning and ending your stitches as you would for traditional hand quilting.

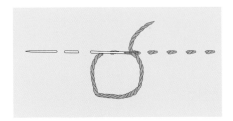

Machine Quilting

For detailed machine-quilting instructions, refer to *Machine Quilting Made Easy!* by Maurine Noble (Martingale & Company, 1994).

I have many of my projects machine quilted in a swirling design I created as an alternative to stippling. It's a wonderful choice as an overall quilting pattern or as a filler for background areas,

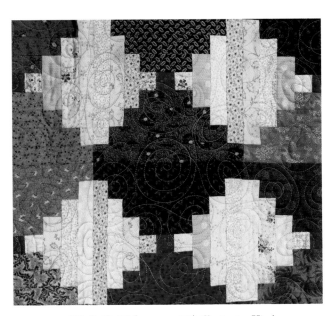

"Taffy Pull" (see page 97) illustrates Kim's swirling pattern stitched by machine.

and I've even had it stitched on top of appliqué motifs with great results. To create this versatile design, sew a free-form circle of any size and then fill in the center with ever-reducing concentric circles (think cinnamon rolls). When you arrive at the center, stitch a gentle wavy line to the next area you want to swirl and continue until the block or top is complete.

Start here.

Binding

A traditional French-fold binding made from 2½"-wide strips is commonly used to finish most quilts. When I bind my quilts, however, I prefer a more unconventional method using 2"-wide strips that results in a traditional look from the front while producing a "chubby" border of color to frame the backing. The yardages for each project will accommodate either method, with enough binding to encircle the quilt perimeter plus approximately 10" for mitered corners.

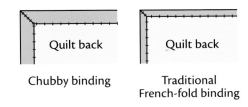

Quilt back   Quilt back

Chubby binding   Traditional
French-fold binding

Traditional French–Fold Binding

1. With right sides together, join the 2½"-wide strips end to end at right angles, stitching diagonally across the corners, to make one long strip. Trim the seam allowances to ¼" and press them open.

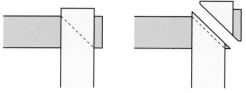

2. Cut one end at a 45° angle and press it under ¼". Fold the strip in half lengthwise, wrong sides together, and press. If the quilt will include a hanging sleeve for display purposes, refer to "Making a Hanging Sleeve" on page 21 and add it prior to binding the quilt. The binding will encase the raw edges of the sleeve.

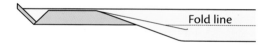

Fold line

3. Beginning along one side of the quilt top, not at a corner, use a ¼" seam to stitch the binding along the raw edges. Stop sewing ¼" from the first corner and backstitch. Clip the thread and remove the quilt from under the presser foot.

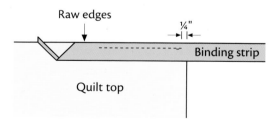

Raw edges

¼"

Binding strip

Quilt top

4. Make a fold in the binding, bringing it up and then back down onto itself to square the corner. Rotate the quilt 90° and reposition it under the presser foot. Resume sewing at the top edge of the quilt, continuing around the perimeter in this manner.

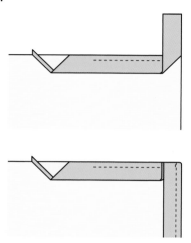

5. When you approach your starting point, cut the end at an angle 1" longer than needed and tuck it inside the sewn binding. Complete the stitching. The raw end will be encased within the binding.

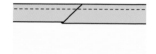

6. Bring the folded edge of the binding to the back of the quilt, enclosing the raw edges. Use a blind stitch and matching thread to hand sew the binding to the back. At each corner, fold the binding to form a miter and stitch it in place.

"Chubby" Binding

For this method, you'll need a bias-tape maker designed to produce 1"-wide, double-fold tape. For scrappy bindings pieced from many lengths, I usually join the strips end to end using a straight seam and start with a straight rather than diagonal fold at the beginning.

1. Cut the strips 2" wide and join them end to end.

2. Slide the pieced strip through the bias-tape maker, pressing the folds with a hot iron as they emerge so the raw edges meet in the center. As the tape emerges from the tape maker, the seams where the strips are joined will automatically be pressed to one side.

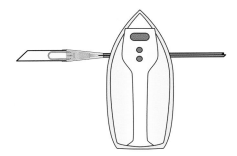

3. Open the fold of the strip along the top edge only. Turn the beginning raw end under ½" and finger-press. Starting along one side of the quilt top, not a corner, align the unfolded raw edge of the binding with the raw edge of the quilt and stitch as instructed in steps 3 and 4 of the French-fold method on page 20.

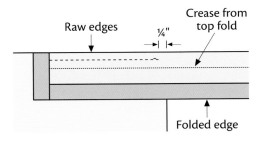

Raw edges   ¼"   Crease from top fold

Folded edge

4. When you approach your starting point, cut the end to extend 1" beyond the folded edge and complete the stitching.

5. Bring the folded edge of the binding to the back and hand stitch it as instructed in step 6 of the French-fold method on page 20. The raw end of the strip will be encased within the binding.

Making a Hanging Sleeve

A hanging sleeve provides the most efficient way of displaying your quilt on a wall, and it can be made from leftover quilt fabrics or muslin. The following steps will enable you to attach a sleeve as the binding is sewn to the quilt.

1. Cut an 8"-wide strip about 2" shorter than the width of your quilt. Fold the short ends under twice, measuring approximately ¼" with each fold. Machine stitch the folds.

2. Fold the strip in half lengthwise, wrong sides together. Center and baste it to the back of the quilt, positioning the raw edges flush with the top raw edge of the quilt. As the binding is stitched, the edges of the sleeve will be permanently attached. Use matching thread to blindstitch the bottom of the sleeve to the quilt back.

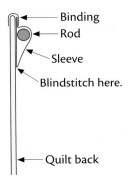

Binding
Rod
Sleeve
Blindstitch here.

Quilt back

Attaching a Quilt Label

Remember to sign and date your quilt using a fabric label, or create your own unique label by adding a muslin border to a small orphan block.

To stabilize the fabric for writing, iron the waxy side of a piece of freezer paper to the wrong side of the fabric. Once you've written the label, remove the paper, press the raw edges under ¼", and pin the label to the quilt back. Use a small dot of liquid basting glue in the seam allowance at each corner to anchor the label and hand stitch it to the back of the quilt.

COUNTRY WEDDING RING

WREATHS OF BLOSSOMING POSIES AND LEAVES ENCIRCLE SIMPLE CHECKERBOARD BLOCKS FOR AN INFORMAL TWIST ON THE MUCH-LOVED WEDDING RING DESIGN. STITCH SOME POSIES OF YOUR OWN AND BRING A BREATH OF FRESH COUNTRY AIR INTO YOUR HOME THROUGHOUT SPRING AND BEYOND.

Materials for Lap Quilt

12 fat quarters (18" x 22") of assorted medium and light prints for blocks, middle border, appliqués, and binding

2¾ yards of cream print for blocks and setting squares

1¾ yards of turquoise print for borders

1 yard of medium green print or equivalent scraps for vines

⅓ yard of muted tan print for flower appliqués

Scraps of assorted green prints for leaf appliqués

3½ yards of fabric for backing

63" x 63" square of batting

⅜" bias bar

Water-soluble marker

Liquid basting glue

Green embroidery floss

Size 5 embroidery needle

Cutting

Cut all strips across the width of fabric unless otherwise noted. Refer to page 29 for appliqué patterns A–C and to "Invisible Machine Appliqué" on page 9 for pattern piece preparation.

From *each* of the 12 fat quarters, cut:
5 strips, 1¾" x 18" (60 total)

From the remainder of the fat quarters, cut a *total* of:
80 squares, 1¾" x 1¾"
36 using pattern B
Enough 2½"-wide random lengths to make a 238" length of binding when joined end to end

From the cream print, cut:
31 strips, 1¾" x 42"; crosscut into:
   • 60 strips, 1¾" x 18"
   • 80 squares, 1¾" x 1¾"
24 squares, 6¾" x 6¾"

From the *bias grain* of the medium green print, cut:
9 strips, 1¼" x 30"

From the remainder of the medium green print and assorted green prints, cut:
108 using pattern C

From the tan print, cut:
36 using pattern A

From the *lengthwise grain* of the turquoise print, cut:
2 strips, 3" x 44¼"
2 strips, 3" x 49¼"
2 strips, 3" x 51¾"
2 strips, 3" x 56¾"

Piecing the Blocks

1. Select five matching medium print 1¾" x 18" strips and five cream print 1¾" x 18" strips and join them to make one each of strip sets A and B. Press the seam allowances toward the medium print. Cut each strip set into the number of 1¾"-wide segments indicated.

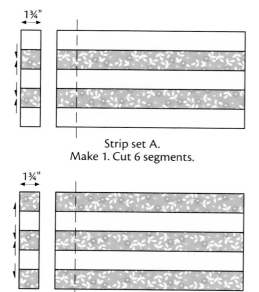

Strip set A.
Make 1. Cut 6 segments.

Strip set B.
Make 1. Cut 4 segments.

2. Lay out three A segments and two B segments to form a Checkerboard block. Join the rows. Press the seam allowances toward the B rows. Repeat for a total of two blocks.

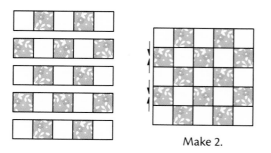

Make 2.

3. Repeat steps 1 and 2 for a total of 24 Checkerboard blocks.

Designed, pieced, and machine appliquéd by Kim Diehl. Machine quilted by Celeste Freiberg.

Finished quilt: 56¾" x 56¾" ❀ Finished block: 6¼" x 6¼"

4. From the remainder of one matching A and B strip set, cut three 1¾"-wide segments from strip set A and two 1¾"-wide segments from strip set B. Make one additional block for a total of 25 Checkerboard blocks measuring 6¾" square.

Piecing the Quilt Center Units

1. Lay out five Checkerboard blocks and four cream print 6¾" setting squares to form a nine-patch unit. Join the pieces in each row. Press the seam allowances toward the cream print. Join the rows. Press the seam allowances toward the middle row. Repeat for a total of four nine-patch units.

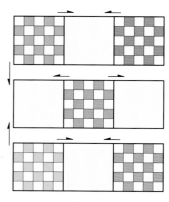

Make 4.

2. Join a cream print 6¾" setting square to the opposite sides of one of the remaining Checkerboard blocks. Press the seam allowances toward the cream print. Repeat for a total of two pieced rectangle units.

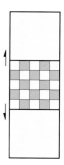

Make 2.

3. Join four cream print 6¾" setting squares with three Checkerboard blocks to form a pieced center row. Press the seam allowances toward the cream print.

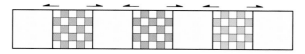

Make 1.

Appliquéing and Assembling the Quilt Center

1. Referring to "Making Bias-Tube Stems and Vines" on page 12, prepare the medium green print 1¼" x 30" strips.

2. Referring to "Preparing Pattern Templates" on page 9, use the pattern on page 29 to make a template of the wreath guide.

3. Select a nine-patch unit and position the straight edge of the wreath guide on the seam line of the center Checkerboard block, centering it from side to side. Use a water-soluble marker or mechanical pencil to lightly trace the curved edge. Repeat for each edge of the checkerboard block to form a wreath shape.

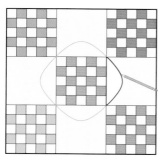

4. Dot the drawn line with liquid basting glue. Beginning at a block corner intersection, press a prepared stem onto the background, centering it on the marked line. Referring to "Stitching the Appliqués" on page 12, stitch the stem in place.

5. Referring to the quilt photo, lay out and stitch the C appliqués. Remove the paper pattern pieces as instructed in "Removing Paper Pattern Pieces" on page 14. Stitch the A and B appliqués, working from the bottom layer to the top, and removing the paper pattern pieces before adding each new layer.

6. Repeat steps 3–5 for a total of four appliquéd nine-patch units.

7. Join an appliquéd nine-patch unit to each side of a pieced rectangle unit. Press the seam allowances toward the pieced rectangle unit. Repeat for a total of two quilt center units.

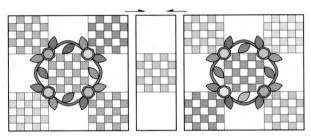

Make 2.

8. Referring to steps 3–5, appliqué a wreath around the center checkerboard block of each quilt center unit.

9. Join the appliquéd units from step 8 to each side of the pieced quilt center row. Press the seam allowances toward the center row. Appliqué a wreath around each remaining checkerboard block. The quilt center should now measure 44¼" square.

Adding the Borders

1. Join a turquoise print 3" x 44¼" strip to the right and left sides of the quilt center. Press the seam allowances toward the turquoise print.

Join a turquoise print 3" x 49¼" strip to the remaining sides of the quilt center. Press the seam allowances toward the turquoise print.

2. Join 20 cream print 1¾" squares and 19 assorted medium print 1¾" squares in alternating positions to form a checkerboard strip. Press the seam allowances toward the assorted prints. Repeat for a total of two checkerboard strips for the side borders. In the same manner, join 21 medium print squares and 20 cream print squares, repeating for a total of two top/bottom borders.

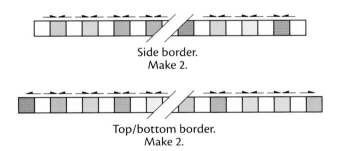

Side border.
Make 2.

Top/bottom border.
Make 2.

3. Join the checkerboard side borders from step 2 to the right and left sides of the quilt top. Press the seam allowances toward the checkerboard border. Join the top and bottom checkerboard borders to the remaining sides of the quilt top. Press the seam allowances toward the checkerboard border.

4. Referring to the quilt diagram on page 28, join a turquoise print 3" x 51¾" strip to the right and left sides of the quilt top. Press the seam allowances toward the turquoise print. Join a turquoise print 3" x 56¾" strip to the remaining sides of the quilt top. Press the seam allowances toward the turquoise print. The pieced quilt top should now measure 56¾" square.

Completing the Quilt

Refer to "Finishing Techniques" on page 17 for details as needed. Layer the quilt top, batting, and backing. Quilt the layers. The background areas of the featured quilt were machine quilted with an assortment of textures, and Xs were stitched in the backgrounds of the checkerboard blocks and middle border. Serpentine feathered cables were quilted in the turquoise borders. Referring to "French Knots" on page 16, use two strands of green embroidery floss and a size 5 embroidery needle to stitch several knots in the center of each flower, tying off and burying the ends within the quilt layers. Join the 2½"-wide random lengths of assorted medium and light prints into one length and use it to bind the quilt.

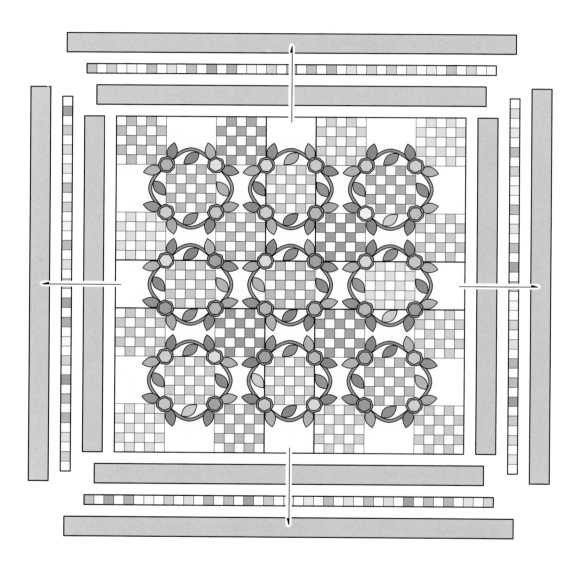

French knots have been added to the center of each flower.

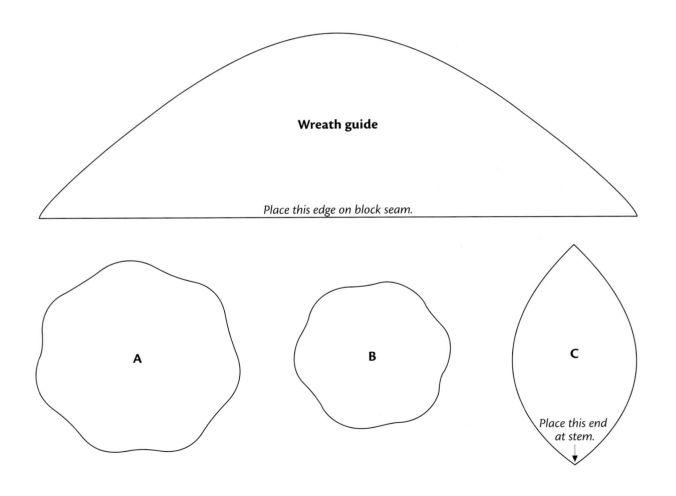

Wreath guide

Place this edge on block seam.

A

B

C

*Place this end
at stem.*

Patterns do not include seam allowances.
Add ¼" to patterns for appliqué
with turned-under edges.

TULIPS AND TOSSED GREENS

SPRING HAS SPRUNG IN THIS WHIMSICAL TABLE RUNNER ADORNED WITH LEAPING RABBITS, FLUTTERING VINES OF BLOOMING YO-YOS, AND SUN-KISSED TULIPS. BRIGHTEN ANY TABLETOP WITH THIS CHEERFUL LITTLE QUILT AS YOU CELEBRATE THE ARRIVAL OF BALMY DAYS AND CLEAR BLUE SKIES.

Materials for Table Runner

1½ yards *total* of assorted prints for yo-yos and tulip appliqués

1⅛ yards of light green print for border and binding

⅝ yard *total* of assorted cream prints for blocks and side setting triangles

1 fat quarter (18" x 22") of brown print for rabbit appliqués

1 fat quarter of medium green plaid for vine and leaf appliqués

Scraps of assorted green prints for leaf appliqués

1⅓ yards of fabric for backing

30" x 47" piece of batting

#8 perle cotton in a neutral color

Size 5 embroidery needle

Liquid basting glue

Straw appliqué needle

Thread to match yo-yos

¼" bias bar

Cutting

Cut all strips across the width of the fabric unless otherwise noted. Refer to page 35 for appliqué patterns A–E and to "Invisible Machine Appliqué" on page 9 for pattern piece preparation.

From the assorted cream prints, cut a *total* of:
13 squares, 4½" x 4½"
14 setting triangles using the template on page 33

From the light green print, cut:
2 strips, 6¼" x 28⅝"
2 strips, 6¼" x 23¼"
4 strips, 2½" x 42" (binding)

From the assorted prints, cut a *total* of:
28 using pattern A
102 using pattern B
10 using pattern D

From the brown print, cut:
2 using pattern C

From the *bias grain* of the medium green plaid, cut:
Enough 1"-wide lengths to make four 36"-long strips when joined end to end
6 strips, 1¼" x 4"

From the remainder of the medium green plaid and the assorted green print scraps, cut a *total* of:
40 using pattern E

Piecing the Quilt Top

1. Arrange the cream print squares and setting triangles into five diagonal rows. Join the pieces in each row. Press the seam allowances open. Trim away the dog-ear points. Join the rows. Press the seam allowances open.

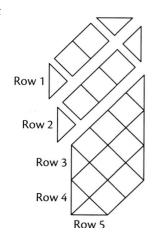

Row 1
Row 2
Row 3
Row 4
Row 5

2. Sew the remaining setting triangles into pairs to make two corner units. Press the seam allowances open. Trim away the dog-ear points. Add a corner unit to the top left and bottom right corners of the quilt center. Press the seam allowances open.

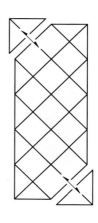

3. Join a light green print 6¼" x 28⅝" strip to the right and left sides of the quilt center. Press the seam allowances toward the green print. Join a light green print 6¼" x 23¼" strip to the remaining sides of the quilt center. Press the seam allowances toward the green print. The pieced quilt top should now measure 23¼" x 40⅛".

Making the Yo-Yos

1. Select an A circle. With the wrong side up, turn a portion of the edge toward you ⅛" to create a hem. Using a knotted length of perle cotton and the size 5 embroidery needle, bring the needle up through the hem from the wrong side of the folded fabric to bury the knot between the layers. Sew a running stitch through all of the layers, close to the folded edge. Continue turning the hem to the back and stitching as you work your way around the circle to your starting position; do not cut the thread. Gently pull the threaded needle to gather the yo-yo edges into the center. Insert the needle just to the side of the center, under the gathered edge, and bring it out on the back of the yo-yo. Knot and clip the thread from the back, keeping the gathers taut. Repeat for a total of 28 large yo-yos.

Designed, pieced, and hand and machine appliquéd by Kim Diehl.
Machine quilted by Celeste Freiberg, with hand-quilted accents by Kim Diehl.

Finished quilt: 23¼" x 40⅛" ❀ **Finished block:** 4" x 4"

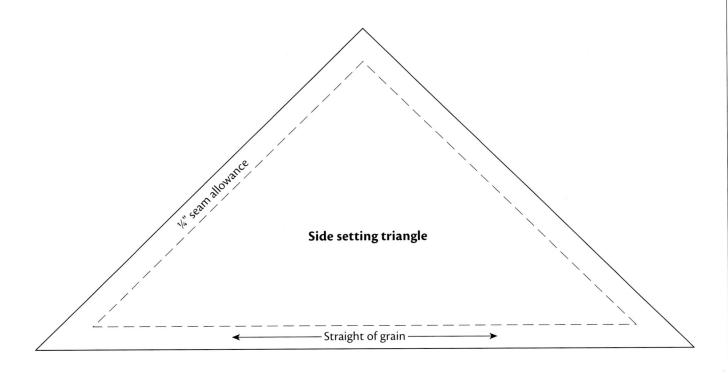

2. Repeat step 1 with the B circles for a total of 102 small yo-yos.

Appliquéing the Quilt Top

1. Center a large yo-yo on each corner of the cream squares and at the points of each setting triangle. When you're pleased with their placement, use two or three drops of liquid basting glue to anchor each yo-yo in place.

2. Position two small yo-yos on the cream print seam lines (but not on the border edges), centering them to fill the spaces between the large yo-yos. When you're pleased with their placement, anchor the small yo-yos with liquid basting glue. Reserve the remaining 22 small yo-yos.

3. Referring to "Turn-Free Hand Appliqué" on page 15, use the straw needle and matching thread to stitch the yo-yos in place.

4. Position a prepared C appliqué onto one long side of the border as shown; baste. Referring to "Stitching the Appliqués" on page 12, stitch the appliqué in place, leaving small openings as shown so the vines can be added later. Repeat on the opposite border. Referring to "Removing Paper Pattern Pieces" on page 14, remove the paper pattern pieces from the rabbits.

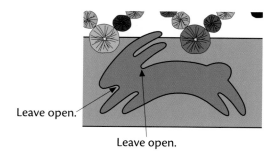

Leave open.

Leave open.

5. Referring to "Making Bias-Tube Stems and Vines" on page 12, prepare the green plaid 36" and 4" bias lengths using a very scant ¼" seam allowance. Turn one end of each 4" stem under about ¼" and anchor it with liquid basting glue.

6. Using the quilt photo as a guide, lay out and baste a prepared 36" vine, tucking one raw end under a rabbit opening and shaping the vine to flow around the border corner; trim any unnecessary length. In the same manner, lay out and baste a second prepared vine, tucking one raw end under the remaining rabbit opening. Stitch the vines. Appliqué the unstitched areas of the rabbit. Repeat with the remaining rabbit appliqué.

7. Referring to the quilt photo, work from the bottom layer to the top to lay out and stitch nine reserved yo-yos, 15 prepared E appliqués, and four prepared D appliqués along the vines of one rabbit. Remember to remove the paper pattern pieces before adding each new layer. Repeat with the remaining rabbit appliqué.

8. In each open border corner, lay out, baste, and stitch three green plaid 4" bias stems as shown. To the stems in each corner, stitch four prepared E appliqués, two reserved yo-yos, and one D appliqué.

Completing the Quilt

Refer to "Finishing Techniques" on page 17 for details as needed. Layer the quilt top, batting, and backing. Quilt the layers. The featured quilt was machine quilted with a teardrop medallion in the center of each cream print square and half medallions in the side setting triangles. The background areas of the border were quilted with a tiny stipple, and the teardrop design was repeated in the open area in front of each rabbit. The border vines and appliqués were outlined with a hand-quilting stitch to emphasize their shapes and the enclosed vine curves were machine quilted with a repeating pattern of straight lines. Join the four 2½"-wide light green print strips into one length and use it to bind the quilt.

Patterns do not include
seam allowances.
Add ¼" to patterns
for appliqué with
turned-under edges.

C

D

E

A

B

TEA WITH GRANDMA

TRADITIONAL BLOCKS IN SUNNY SPRING
COLORS BRING TO MIND MEMORIES OF
AFTERNOON NAPS ON GRANDMA'S FLUFFY BED,
UNDER CRISPLY IRONED LINENS AND SOFTLY
WORN QUILTS.

Materials for Bed Quilt

4⅜ yards of celery green print for blocks and border

3 yards *total* of assorted pink prints* for blocks,
    border, and binding

2½ yards *total* of assorted lavender, butterscotch,
    sage green, and blue prints for blocks and border

5⅓ yards of fabric for backing

81" x 96" piece of batting

*For color depth, stretch your range from pale pink
to deep rose.*

Cutting

Cut all strips across the width of the fabric unless otherwise noted.

From the celery green print, cut:

11 strips, 2⅜" x 42"; crosscut into 176 squares, 2⅜" x 2⅜". Cut each square in half diagonally once to yield 352 triangles.

19 strips, 2" x 42"; crosscut into:
- 176 rectangles, 2" x 3½"
- 44 squares, 2" x 2"

16 strips, 3½" x 42"; crosscut into 176 squares, 3½" x 3½"

8 strips, 2½" x 42"; crosscut into 128 squares, 2½" x 2½"

From 1 of the assorted pink prints, cut the following pieces for 1 set:

2 squares, 3⅞" x 3⅞"; cut each square in half diagonally once to yield 4 triangles (176 total)

5 squares, 2" x 2" (220 total)

Repeat to cut a total of 44 sets. Keep the pieces from each set together.

From the remainder of the pink prints, cut a *total* of:

8 rectangles, 3" x 8"

16 rectangles, 2" x 8"

16 rectangles, 1½" x 8"

Enough 2½"-wide random lengths to make a 340" length of binding when joined end to end

From the assorted lavender, butterscotch, sage green, and blue prints, cut 44 matching sets of:

4 rectangles, 2" x 3½" (176 total)

From the remainder of the lavender, butterscotch, sage green, and blue prints, cut a *total* of:

24 rectangles, 3" x 8"

48 rectangles, 2" x 8"

48 rectangles, 1½" x 8"

Piecing the Grandmother's Choice Blocks

1. Select a matching set of pink print 3⅞" triangles and 2" squares. Join one short side of a celery print 2⅜" triangle to one of the 2" squares. Press the seam allowance toward the celery print. Sew a second celery print triangle to the adjacent side of the square. Press the seam allowance toward the celery print. Trim away the dog-ear points. Repeat for a total of four pieced triangles.

Make 4.

2. Join a 3⅞" triangle to each pieced triangle from step 1. Press the seam allowances toward the pink print triangle.

Make 4.

3. Sew a unit from step 2 to each long side of a celery print 2" x 3½" rectangle, placing the units in mirror-image positions. Press the seam allowances toward the celery print. Repeat for a total of two row units.

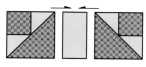

Make 2.

4. Join a celery print 2" x 3½" rectangle to opposite sides of a pink print 2" square. Press the seam allowances toward the celery print.

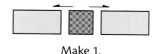

Make 1.

Designed by Kim Diehl. Pieced by Deslynn Mecham, Pat Peyton, and Kim Diehl.
Machine quilted by Celeste Freiberg.

Finished quilt: 75½" x 90½" 🌸 **Finished block: 7½" x 7½"**

5. Lay out the pieced units from steps 3 and 4 in three horizontal rows. Join the rows. Press the seam allowances toward the middle row.

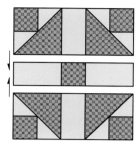

6. Repeat steps 1–5 for a total of 44 Grandmother's Choice blocks measuring 8" square.

Piecing the Nine-Patch Variation Blocks

1. Select a matching set of 2" x 3½" rectangles cut from the assorted lavender, butterscotch, sage green, and blue prints. Join a celery print 3½" square to opposite sides of an assorted-print rectangle. Press the seam allowances toward the celery print. Repeat for a total of two row units.

Make 2.

2. Join the remaining two assorted-print rectangles to opposite sides of a celery print 2" square. Press the seam allowances toward the celery print.

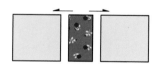

Make 1.

3. Lay out the pieced units from steps 1 and 2 in three horizontal rows. Join the rows. Press the seam allowances away from the middle row

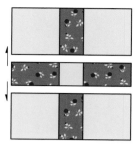

4. Repeat steps 1–3 for a total of 44 Nine-Patch variation blocks measuring 8" square.

Assembling the Quilt Center

1. Lay out four Grandmother's Choice blocks and four Nine-Patch variation blocks in alternating positions to form a row. Join the blocks. Press the seam allowances toward the Nine-Patch blocks. Repeat for a total of 11 pieced rows.

Make 11 rows.

2. Lay out the rows in alternating directions. Join the rows. Press the seam allowances open. The pieced quilt center should now measure 60½" x 83".

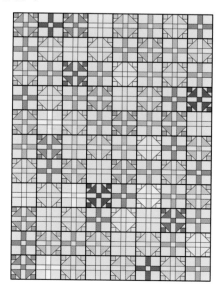

Piecing the Border Blocks

1. Randomly select two assorted print 1½" x 8" rectangles, two assorted print 2" x 8" rectangles, and one assorted print 3" x 8" rectangle. Join the pieces to form a pieced square unit. Press the seam allowances away from the center rectangle.

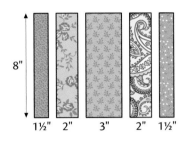

2. Use a pencil to draw a diagonal line on the wrong side of each celery print 2½" square. With right sides together, layer a marked square over each corner of the pieced units from step 1. Stitch the layered corners exactly on the drawn lines. Press and trim as instructed in "Pressing Triangle Units" on page 9. Repeat for a total of 32 border blocks measuring 8" square.

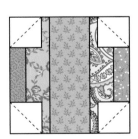

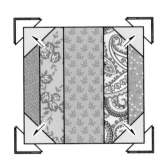

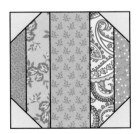

Make 32.

Assembling and Adding the Borders

1. With the rectangles positioned vertically, join 11 border blocks end to end. Press the seam allowances in one direction. Repeat for a total of two side borders. Sew the borders to the right and left sides of the quilt center. Press the seam allowances toward the borders.

2. In the same manner, join the remaining 10 border blocks. Add the border to the bottom side of the quilt center. Press the seam allowances toward the border.

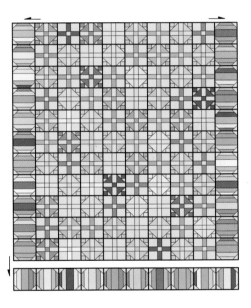

Completing the Quilt

Refer to "Finishing Techniques" on page 17 for details as needed. Layer the quilt top, batting, and backing. Quilt the layers. The center of the featured quilt was machine quilted in an allover pattern of free-form stems adorned with feathers and curlicue circles, with whimsical shapes and lines filling in the areas around them. The background triangles in the border were quilted with arced lines, and the rectangles were stitched with running serpentine feathered vines. Join the 2½"-wide random lengths of assorted pink print strips into one length and use it to bind the quilt.

SPRING RECIPES

CLUB SALAD

*Take all the ingredients of a classic club sandwich and toss them with your favorite
mixed greens for this refreshing spring salad.*

Torn mixed greens (I use iceberg and red-leaf lettuce with a bit of baby spinach)
⅓ pound thinly sliced deli turkey, julienned
⅓ pound thinly sliced deli ham, julienned
⅓ pound thinly sliced roast beef, julienned
6 slices cooked bacon, crumbled
2 medium tomatoes, cut into eighths
1 cup diced cheddar cheese
1 bunch green onions, sliced, white and some green parts

Fill a large serving bowl about two-thirds full of torn greens. Mound the deli meats in three rows over
the center of the greens, leaving room around the outside edge for the remaining ingredients. Surround
the meat with bacon bits. Lay tomato wedges around the inner edge of the bowl, leaving an equal amount
of space between each one; fill the spaces with cheese. Sprinkle green onions over the entire salad. Serve
with croutons and your favorite dressing.

PENNE PRIMAVERA

Fresh, crisp asparagus and baby peas give this pasta dish all the flavors of spring. Stir in cooked shrimp or chicken breast pieces for a quick and easy one-dish meal.

1 cup chicken broth
1 tablespoon cornstarch
8 ounces uncooked penne pasta
1 to 2 tablespoons olive oil
1 bunch fresh asparagus, cut into 1" pieces
4 green onions, sliced, white and some green parts
3 cloves garlic, minced
1 package (6 ounces) frozen baby peas
1 tablespoon dried parsley
¼ cup shredded Parmesan cheese

Whisk together the chicken broth and cornstarch; set aside. Cook the pasta according to the package instructions; drain well and set aside.

Meanwhile, pour the olive oil into a large preheated skillet. Add the asparagus and stir-fry over medium-high heat for about 2 minutes, until crisp-tender. Add the green onions and garlic and cook another minute, stirring constantly. Gently stir in the peas, cooking just until warmed. Add the broth mixture, stirring until bubbly and slightly thickened. Stir in the cooked pasta and parsley. Season to taste with salt and freshly ground pepper. Top with the Parmesan cheese and serve.

CINNAMON SPICE BANANA MUFFINS

Inspired by my mother-in-law's delicious banana bread, these muffins with their buttery, spiced tops, and soft, cakelike centers, are my daughters' all-time favorites!

Batter

¾ cup sugar
½ cup packed brown sugar
¼ pound (1 stick) butter, softened
⅓ cup sour cream
3 eggs
2 cups flour
2 teaspoons baking soda
½ teaspoon salt
3 medium ripe bananas, mashed

Topping

4 tablespoons (½ stick) butter, melted
½ cup sugar
2 teaspoons ground cinnamon

Preheat the oven to 350°. In a large mixing bowl, cream together the sugars, butter, and sour cream. Add the eggs one at a time, mixing well after each addition. In a small bowl, stir together the flour, baking soda, and salt. Add the flour mixture to the wet ingredients in three additions. Add the bananas, mixing just until blended. Spoon the batter into paper-lined muffin tins, filling each about two-thirds full. Bake approximately 20 to 30 minutes or until the tops are nicely mounded and very lightly browned.

Stir the sugar and cinnamon together in a small bowl. When the muffins are cool enough to handle, dip the tops in melted butter, then in the cinnamon-sugar mixture.

Makes approximately 24 muffins.

REMEMBRANCE

PRESERVE AND HONOR OUR QUILTING
HERITAGE WHEN YOU STITCH THIS
TRADITIONAL QUILT SAMPLER COMPOSED
OF LARGE, VINTAGE-
STYLE BLOCKS LOVED
AND HELD DEAR IN YOUR
GRANDMOTHER'S ERA.
CHOOSE YOUR FAVORITE
COLOR AND LET IT SHINE
OR SELECT A VARIETY
OF PRINTS FOR A BIT OF
MODERN CHARM.

Materials for Lap Quilt

5⅝ yards of blue print for blocks, borders, and binding

3½ yards of cream print for blocks and borders

4¾ yards of fabric for backing

84" x 84" square of batting

⅜" bias bar

Water-soluble marker

Liquid basting glue

Cutting

Cut all strips across the width of the fabric unless otherwise noted.

From the *lengthwise grain* of the blue print, cut:

4 strips, 5½" x 68½"

5 strips, 2½" x 72" (binding)

From the remainder of the blue print, cut:

3 strips, 3⅞" x 42"; crosscut into 30 squares, 3⅞" x 3⅞"

4 strips, 3½" x 42"; crosscut into:
- 16 squares, 3½" x 3½"
- 12 rectangles, 3½" x 7"

1 strip, 6¼" x 42"; crosscut into 5 squares, 6¼" x 6¼"

2 strips, 2" x 42"

20 strips, 2½" x 42"; reserving 1 strip, crosscut 19 strips into:
- 24 strips, 2½" x 16"
- 24 rectangles, 2½" x 5½"
- 24 rectangles, 2½" x 4½"
- 24 rectangles, 2½" x 3½"
- 16 squares, 2½" x 2½"

4 strips, 1½" x 42"; reserving 3 strips, crosscut 1 strip into 20 squares, 1½" x 1½"

1 strip, 5⅞" x 42"; crosscut into 4 squares, 5⅞" x 5⅞". Cut each square in half diagonally once to yield 8 triangles.

3 strips, 3⅜" x 42"; crosscut into 24 squares, 3⅜" x 3⅜". Cut each square in half diagonally once to yield 48 triangles.

1 rectangle, 7½" x 21". From the rectangle, cut 8 bias strips, 1¼" wide.

From the cream print, cut:

3 strips, 3⅞" x 42"; crosscut into 30 squares, 3⅞" x 3⅞"

3 strips, 3½" x 42"; crosscut into:
- 30 squares, 3½" x 3½"
- 1 rectangle, 3½" x 9½"

1 strip, 6¼" x 42"; crosscut into 5 squares, 6¼" x 6¼"

15 strips, 2½" x 42"; reserving 1 strip, crosscut 14 strips into:
- 24 rectangles, 2½" x 4"
- 24 rectangles, 2½" x 5"
- 24 rectangles, 2½" x 6"
- 16 rectangles, 2½" x 7"

4 strips, 2" x 42"; reserving 2 strips, crosscut 2 strips into 24 squares, 2" x 2"

10 strips, 1½" x 42"; reserving 3 strips, crosscut 7 strips into:
- 12 strips, 1½" x 16"
- 16 rectangles, 1½" x 6"

2 strips, 5⅞" x 42"; crosscut into 8 squares, 5⅞" x 5⅞". Cut each square in half diagonally once to yield 16 triangles. Trim the remainder of the strip to 3" wide and cut 7 squares, 3" x 3".

1 strip, 3" x 42"; crosscut into 9 squares, 3" x 3"

2 strips, 3⅜" x 42"; crosscut into 16 squares, 3⅜" x 3⅜"

1 strip, 6" x 42"; crosscut into 4 squares, 6" x 6"

Piecing the Half-Square-Triangle Units

1. Use a pencil to draw a diagonal line on the wrong side of the cream print 6¼" squares. With right sides together, layer a marked square with a blue print 6¼" square. Stitch ¼" from each side of the drawn line. Cut the joined pair apart on the drawn line. Press the two resulting half-square-triangle units open, with the seam allowance toward the blue print. Trim away the dog-ear points. Repeat for a total of 10 large half-square-triangle units. You will use these for the Chain and Hourglass blocks.

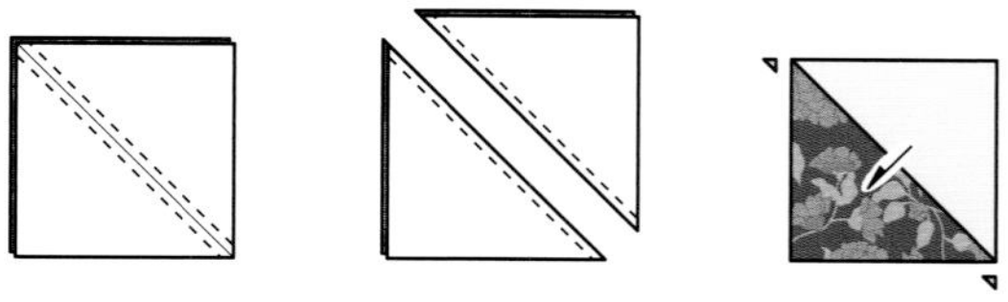

Make 10.

Designed, pieced, and machine appliquéd by Kim Diehl. Machine quilted by Celeste Freiberg.

Finished quilt: 78½" x 78½" ✿ **Finished block: 15" x 15"**

2. Repeat step 1 using the cream print and blue print 3⅞" squares for a total of 60 medium half-square-triangle units. You will use these for the Double-X Variation blocks, the Geese in the Pond blocks, and the Hearth and Home block.

3. Repeat step 1 using the cream print and blue print 3⅜" squares for a total of 32 small half-square-triangle units. You will use these for the sashing and outer border Pinwheel blocks.

Piecing the Double-X Variation Blocks

1. Lay out five cream print 3½" squares and four blue print 3½" squares in three horizontal rows to make a nine-patch unit. Join the pieces in each row. Press the seam allowances toward the blue print. Join the rows. Press the seam allowances toward the middle row. Repeat for a total of two nine-patch units.

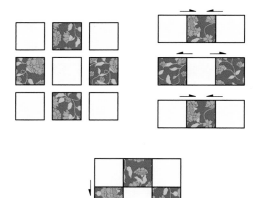

Make 2.

2. Join three medium half-square-triangle units. Press the seam allowances as shown. Repeat for a total of four side units.

Make 4.

3. Join four medium half-square-triangle units. Press the seam allowances as shown. Join a cream print 3½" square to the dark end of the pieced strip. Press the seam allowance toward the cream print. Repeat for a total of four top/bottom units.

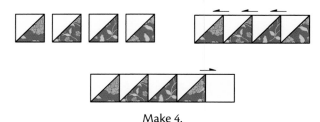

Make 4.

4. Join two side units to opposite sides of each nine-patch unit from step 1. Press the seam allowances toward the nine-patch units. Add a top/bottom unit to the remaining sides of the nine-patch units. Press the seam allowances toward the nine-patch units. Repeat for a total of two Double-X Variation blocks measuring 15½" square.

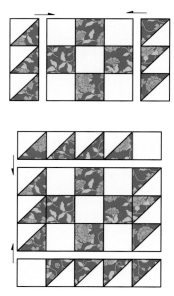

Make 2.

Piecing the Chain and Hourglass Blocks

1. Cut each large half-square-triangle unit in half diagonally once to yield 20 pieced triangle units. Join two pieced triangle units. Press the seam

allowance to one side. Trim away the dog-ear points. Repeat for a total of 10 hourglass units.

Make 10.

2. Join two blue print 2½" x 42" strips and one cream print 2" x 42" strip to form strip set A. Press the seam allowances toward the blue print. Join two cream print 2½" x 42" strips and one blue print 2" x 42" strip to form strip set B. Press the seam allowances toward the blue print. From each strip set, cut four segments, 5½" wide.

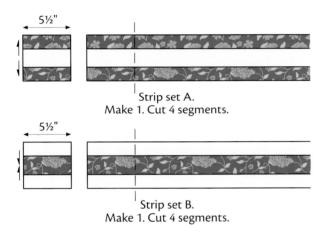

Strip set A.
Make 1. Cut 4 segments.

Strip set B.
Make 1. Cut 4 segments.

3. Lay out five hourglass units, two strip-set A segments, and two strip-set B segments in three horizontal rows to form a block. Join the pieces in each row. Press the seam allowances toward the strip-set segments. Join the rows. Press the seam allowances toward the middle row. Repeat for a total of two Chain and Hourglass blocks measuring 15½" square.

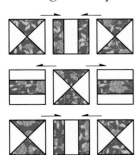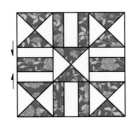

Make 2.

Piecing the Geese in the Pond Blocks

1. Join three blue print and three cream print 1½" x 42" strips as shown to form strip sets C and D. Press the seam allowances toward the blue print. Crosscut strip set C into eight segments, 1½" wide, and eight segments, 3½" wide. Crosscut strip set D into 16 segments, 1½" wide.

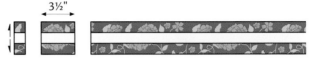

Strip set C.
Make 1. Cut 8 segments, 1½" wide, and 8 segments, 3½" wide.

Strip set D.
Make 1. Cut 16 segments.

2. Using the 1½"-wide segments, lay out one C segment and two D segments to form a nine-patch unit. Join the rows. Press the seam allowances toward the center row. Repeat for a total of eight nine-patch units.

Make 8.

3. Lay out four nine-patch units, four 3½"-wide C segments, and one cream print 3½" square in three horizontal rows to form a center unit. Join the pieces in each row. Press the seam allowances toward the C segments. Join the rows. Press the

seam allowances toward the middle row. Repeat for a total of two pieced center units.

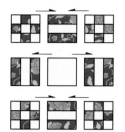 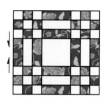

Make 2.

4. Join a medium half-square-triangle unit to opposite sides of a cream print 3½" square as shown. Press the seam allowances toward the half-square-triangle units. Repeat for a total of eight pieced rectangles.

 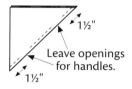

Make 8.

5. Join a pieced rectangle to opposite sides of a pieced center unit. Press the seam allowances toward the center unit. Join a medium half-square triangle to the ends of two remaining pieced rectangles. Press the seam allowances away from the unit center. Join these pieced rectangle units to the remaining edges of the center unit. Press the seam allowances toward the block center. Repeat for a total of two Geese in the Pond blocks measuring 15½" square.

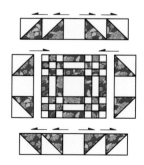 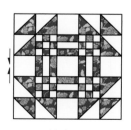

Make 2.

Piecing the Postage Stamp Basket Blocks

1. Referring to "Making Bias-Tube Stems and Vines" on page 12, use a scant ¼" seam allowance to prepare the eight blue print 1¼" x 7½" bias strips.

2. With right sides together, layer a blue print and cream print 5⅞" triangle. Sew along the long bias edges, leaving two 1½"-wide openings about 1½" from each point. Press the seam allowance toward the blue print. Trim away the dog-ear points. Repeat for a total of eight half-square-triangle units.

Leave openings for handles.

1½"

1½"

3. To center the basket handles, use the water-soluble marker to mark a tiny dot at the seam line of the half-square-triangle units, 1½" from each point. Apply small dots of liquid basting glue to the seam allowance of a prepared bias strip. Press the handle onto the cream side of the half-square-triangle unit background to form a basket handle, tucking the ends into the seam openings and aligning the outside edges with the marked dots. (Ensure that you leave at least ½" between the outer curve of the handle and the unit edge to allow for seam allowances.) Trim any excess handle length, leaving a ¼" seam allowance. Sew the openings in the seam closed. Referring to "Stitching the Appliqués" on page 12, stitch the handles in place. Repeat for a total of eight appliquéd basket units.

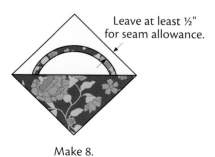

Leave at least ½" for seam allowance.

Make 8.

4. Join a blue print 3⅜" triangle to one end of each of the cream print 3" squares to form eight base units and eight mirror-image base units. Press the seam allowance toward the blue print. Trim away the dog-ear points.

Make 8 of each.

5. Join a base unit to the blue sides of an appliquéd basket unit as shown. Trim away the dog-ear points. Press the seam allowances toward the basket center. If necessary, trim the seam allowance at the point of the basket to ¼". Join a cream print 5⅞" triangle to the bottom edge of the basket unit. Press the seam allowance toward the cream print. Trim away the dog-ear points. Repeat for a total of eight basket units.

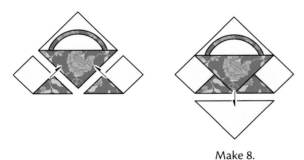

Make 8.

6. Use a pencil to draw a diagonal line on the wrong side of eight blue print 1½" squares. Layer a prepared square over the bottom point of a basket unit. Stitch, press, and trim as instructed in "Pressing Triangle Units" on page 9. Repeat for a total of eight pieced basket units measuring 8" square.

Make 8.

7. Lay out four pieced basket units in two horizontal rows to form a block. Join the units in each row. Press the seam allowances in alternating directions. Join the rows. Press the seam allowance to one side. Repeat for a total of two Postage Stamp Basket blocks measuring 15½" square.

Make 2.

Piecing the Hearth and Home Block

1. Join two blue print 3½" squares to opposite sides of a cream print 3½" square. Press the seam allowances toward the blue prints. Repeat for a total of two pieced strips. Join these strips to each long side of the cream print 3½" x 9½" rectangle. Press the seam allowances away from the center rectangle.

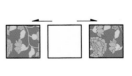 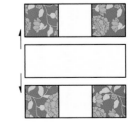

2. Join two medium half-square-triangle units to opposite sides of a blue print 3½" square as shown. Press the seam allowances toward the blue print. Repeat for a total of four pieced

rectangle units. Join two of these units to the right and left sides of the step 1 unit. Press the seam allowances toward the center unit.

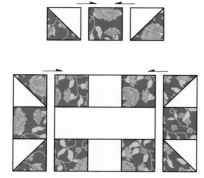

3. Sew a cream print 3½" square to the ends of the remaining pieced rectangle units. Press the seam allowances toward the cream print. Join these units to the remaining sides of the center unit. Press the seam allowances toward the center unit. The pieced Hearth and Home block should measure 15½" square.

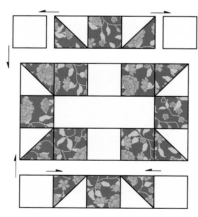

Make 2.

Assembling the Quilt Center

1. Lay out four small half-square-triangle units in two horizontal rows to form a Pinwheel block. Join the units in each row. Press the seam allowances as shown. Join the rows. Press the seam allowances to one side. Repeat for a total of eight Pinwheel blocks measuring 5½" square.

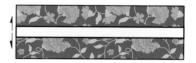

Make 8.

2. Join a blue print 2½" x 16" strip to each long side of a cream print 1½" x 16" strip to form a sashing unit. Press the seam allowances toward the blue print. Trim the unit to measure 15½". Repeat for a total of 12 sashing units.

Make 12.

3. Lay out three sashing units and two Pinwheel blocks in alternating positions. Join the pieces. Press the seam allowances toward the sashing units. Repeat for a total of two pieced sashing rows. Reserve the remaining four Pinwheel blocks for the outer border.

Make 2.

4. Lay out the blocks and remaining sashing units in three horizontal rows as shown. Join the pieces in each row. Press the seam allowances toward the sashing units. Join the block and sashing

rows to form the quilt center. Press the seam allowances toward the sashing rows. The pieced quilt center should now measure 55½" square.

Assembling and Adding the Middle Border

1. Use a pencil to draw a diagonal line on the wrong side of the cream print 2" squares. With right sides together, layer a prepared square over one corner of a blue print 3½" x 7" rectangle. Stitch, press and trim as instructed in "Pressing Triangle Units" on page 9. In the same manner, add a prepared cream print 2" square to the adjacent corner as shown. Repeat for a total of 12 A units.

A unit.
Make 12.

2. Layer a cream print 2½" x 4" rectangle over one end of a blue print 2½" x 5½" rectangle as shown. Use a pencil to lightly mark a diagonal line from

the bottom inner corner of the cream print rectangle to the point of the blue print rectangle underneath. Stitch the pair together exactly on the drawn line. Trim away the excess fabric ¼" from the seam line. Press the seam allowance toward the cream print. Repeat for a total of 12 B units. In the same manner, use the remaining cream print 2½" x 4" rectangles and blue print 2½" x 5½" rectangles to make 12 B mirror-image units as shown.

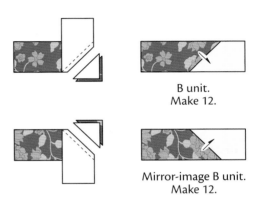

B unit.
Make 12.

Mirror-image B unit.
Make 12.

3. Repeat step 2 using the cream print 2½" x 5" rectangles and blue print 2½" x 4½" rectangles to make 12 C units and 12 C mirror-image units.

4. Repeat step 2 using the cream print 2½" x 6" rectangles and blue print 2½" x 3½" rectangles to make 12 D units and 12 D mirror-image units.

5. Lay out one A unit, one each of the B, C, and D units, and one each of the B, C, and D mirror-image units as shown. Join the pieces. Press the seam allowances away from the A unit. Repeat for a total of 12 delectable-mountain units.

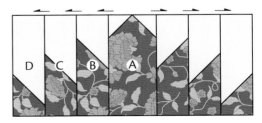

Make 12.

6. Use a pencil to draw a diagonal line on the wrong side of the blue print 2½" squares. Layer a prepared square over one end of a cream print 2½" x 7" rectangle. Sew, press, and trim as instructed in step 1. Repeat for a total of 8 pieced rectangles, and 8 pieced mirror-image rectangles.

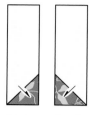

Make 8 of each.

7. Join a blue print 1½" square to one end of a cream print 1½" x 6" rectangle. Press the seam allowance toward the square. Repeat for a total of 12 pieced strips.

Make 12.

8. Lay out a pieced rectangle and a pieced mirror-image rectangle from step 6 with a pieced strip from step 7 as shown. Join the pieces. Press the seam allowances toward the center strip. Repeat for a total of 8 pieced units. Set aside the remaining four pieced strips for use in step 11.

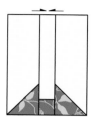

Make 8.

9. Lay out three delectable-mountain units and two pieced units from step 8 as shown. Join the units. Press the seam allowances away from the delectable-mountain units. Repeat for a total of four pieced border rows.

Make 4.

10. Join a pieced border row to the right and left sides of the quilt center. Press the seam allowances away from the quilt center.

11. Join a cream print 1½" x 6" rectangle to one side of a cream print 6" square. Press the seam allowance toward the rectangle. Join a reserved pieced strip from step 8 to the adjacent side of the cream square as shown. Press the seam allowance toward the pieced strip. Repeat for a total of four corner-post units.

Make 4.

12. Join a corner-post unit to each end of the remaining pieced border rows as shown. Press the seam allowances away from the corner posts. Join these rows to the remaining sides of the quilt center. Press the seam allowances away from the quilt center.

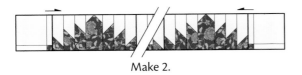

Make 2.

Assembling and Adding the Outer Border

1. Join a blue print 5½" x 68½" strip to the right and left sides of the quilt top. Press the seam allowances toward the outer border.

2. Join the reserved Pinwheel blocks from "Assembling the Quilt Center" to each end of the remaining blue print 5½" x 68½" strips. Press the seam allowances toward the blue print. Join these strips to the remaining sides of the quilt top. Press the seam allowances toward the outer border.

Completing the Quilt Top

Refer to "Finishing Techniques" on page 17 for details as needed. Layer the quilt top, batting, and backing. Quilt the layers. Because this quilt contains many different blocks and shapes, it was machine quilted using a variety of designs. Join the five blue print 2½" x 72" strips into one length and use it to bind the quilt.

LIBERTY

EMBRACE YOUR PATRIOTIC SPIRIT WHEN YOU STITCH THESE CRIMSON PATCHWORK BLOCKS AND MAJESTIC WINGED EAGLES, SO SYMBOLIC OF OUR TREASURED AMERICAN LIBERTY. THIS LITTLE QUILT CELEBRATES THE FREEDOMS ENJOYED BY ONE AND ALL, FROM SEA TO SHINING SEA.

Materials for Quilt

1⅝ yards of neutral print for background

1 fat quarter (18" x 22") *each* of 6 assorted red prints for blocks, flower appliqués, and binding

1 fat quarter *each* of 4 assorted dark blue prints for eagle appliqués

3 fat eighths of assorted green homespuns for leaf appliqués

1 fat quarter (9" x 22") of brown print for stem appliqués

Scraps of assorted gold prints for star and flower appliqués

Scraps of batting for stuffed appliqué embellishments

2⅔ yards of fabric for backing

48" x 48" piece of batting

Liquid basting glue

Cutting

Cut all strips across the width of fabric unless otherwise noted. Refer to pages 62 and 63 for appliqué patterns A–F and to "Invisible Machine Appliqué" on page 9 for pattern piece preparation.

From the neutral print, cut:

4 strips, 9½" x 42"; from *each* strip, cut 1 rectangle, 9½" x 24½", and 1 rectangle, 6½" x 12½"

3 strips, 2⅜" x 42"; crosscut into 48 squares, 2⅜" x 2⅜". Cut each square in half diagonally once to yield 96 triangles.

3 strips, 2" x 42"; crosscut into 48 squares, 2" x 2"

From *each* of the assorted red prints, cut*:

2 squares, 3⅞" x 3⅞"; cut each square in half diagonally once to yield 4 triangles (24 total)

4 squares, 2" x 2" (24 total)

4 squares, 2⅜" x 2⅜"; cut each square in half diagonally once to yield 8 triangles (48 total)

*Keep the red patchwork pieces organized by print to simplify the sewing process.

From the remainder of the red prints, cut a *total* of:

16 using pattern E

Enough 2½"-wide random lengths to make a 188" length of binding when joined end to end

From the brown print, cut:

4 using pattern A

4 using pattern A reversed

From *each* of the assorted dark blue prints, cut:

1 using pattern B (4 total)

From the gold print scraps, cut a *total* of:

12 using pattern C

16 using pattern F

From the assorted green homespuns, cut a *total* of:

24 using pattern D

Piecing the Blocks

1. Select one matching set of red print patchwork pieces. With right sides together, layer a red print and neutral print 2⅜" triangle. Sew along the long bias edges. Press the seam allowance toward the red print. Trim away the dog-ear points. Repeat for a total of four half-square-triangle units.

Make 4.

2. Lay out two half-square-triangle units and two neutral print 2" squares in two horizontal rows. Join the pieces in each row. Press the seam allowances toward the neutral print. Join the rows. Press the seam allowance to one side. Repeat for a total of two small triangle units.

Make 2.

3. Join a neutral print 2⅜" triangle to one side of a red print 2" square. Press the seam allowance toward the neutral print. Sew a second neutral print 2⅜" triangle to the adjacent side of the red print square. Press the seam allowance toward the neutral print. Trim away the dog-ear points. Repeat for a total of two pieced triangles.

Make 2.

Designed, pieced, and machine appliquéd by Kim Diehl.
Machine quilted by Celeste Freiberg, with hand-quilted big-stitch accents by Kim Diehl.

Finished quilt: 42" x 42" ❋ Finished block: 6" x 6"

4. Sew a red print 3⅞" triangle to a pieced triangle from step 3. Press the seam allowance toward the red print. Trim away the dog-ear points. Repeat for a total of two large triangle units.

Make 2.

5. Lay out two small triangle units from step 2 and two large triangle units in two horizontal rows to form a block. Join the units in each row. Press the seam allowances toward the large red triangles. Join the rows. Press the seam allowance to one side.

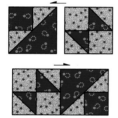 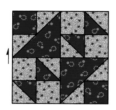

6. Repeat steps 1–5 for a total of 12 blocks measuring 6½" square.

Assembling the Quilt Top

1. Lay out four blocks in two horizontal rows to form the quilt center. Join the blocks in each row. Press the seam allowances in opposite directions. Join the rows. Press the seam allowance to one side.

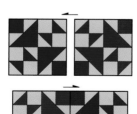

2. Sew a neutral print 6½" x 12½" rectangle to the right and left sides of the quilt center. Press the seam allowances toward the rectangles.

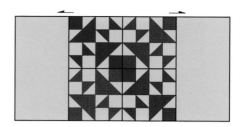

3. Join a pieced block to each end of a neutral print 6½" x 12½" rectangle as shown. Press the seam allowances toward the rectangle. Repeat for a total of two pieced rectangles.

4. Sew a pieced rectangle to the remaining sides of the quilt center unit. Press the seam allowances away from the quilt center.

5. Sew a neutral print 9½" x 24½" rectangle to the right and left sides of the quilt top. Press the seam allowances away from the quilt center.

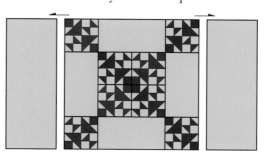

6. Keeping the top edges flush, sew a pieced block to the ends of a neutral print 9½" x 24½" rectangle as shown. Press the seam allowances toward the rectangle. Repeat for a total of two pieced rectangles.

Make 2.

7. Join the long edges of the pieced rectangles from step 6 to the remaining sides of the quilt top. Press the seam allowances away from the quilt center. The pieced quilt top should now measure 42½" square.

Appliquéing the Quilt Top

1. Use an acrylic ruler and a water-soluble marker to mark a 45°-angle line at each outer corner of the neutral print 9½" x 24½" rectangles as shown, measuring from the edge of the adjacent pieced blocks. (The corners of these rectangles will be trimmed later on the marked lines.)

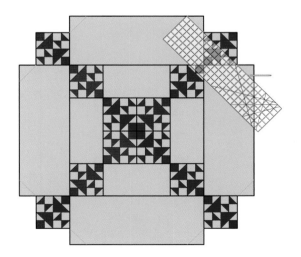

2. Referring to the quilt photo, position and baste an A appliqué, placing the bottom of the stem about ½" from the background raw edge. Referring to "Stitching the Appliqués" on page 12, stitch the stem. Remove the paper pattern piece as instructed in "Removing Paper Pattern Pieces" on page 14. Stitch a reverse appliqué to the background, placing it in a mirror-image position. Repeat for each side of the quilt top.

3. Lay out and stitch one B appliqué, three C appliqués, six D appliqués, and four E and F appliqués to each side of the quilt top. Remember to work from the bottom to the top and remove the paper pattern pieces between each layer.

4. Referring to "Stuffed Appliqués" on page 16, stuff any appliqués that you wish to accent. (On the featured quilt, the stars, leaves, and flower centers were stuffed.)

Completing the Quilt

Refer to "Finishing Techniques" on page 17 for details as needed. Trim away the excess corner fabric on each side of the quilt top, cutting exactly on the drawn lines. Layer the quilt top, batting, and backing. Quilt the layers. The background areas of the featured quilt were machine quilted with a small stipple design. Hand-quilted big-stitch accents were added to the red portion of the patchwork blocks and to the appliqués. The eagles were quilted with free-form circles, lines, and scallops to resemble feathers. Join the 2½"-wide random lengths of assorted red prints into one length and use it to bind the quilt. (This binding measurement includes extra length to accommodate the unique corners and angles.)

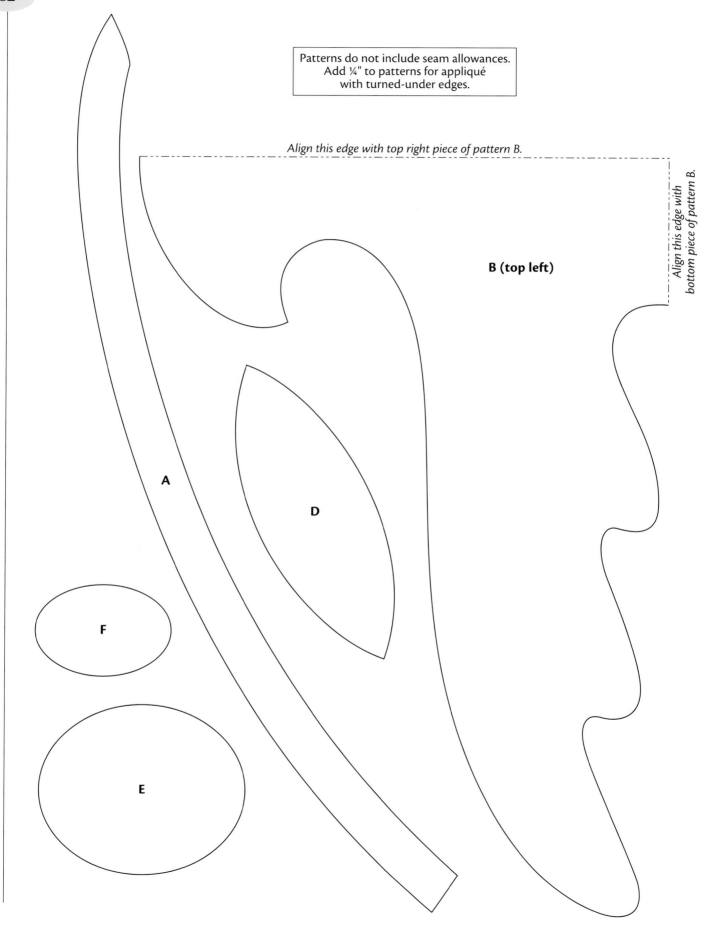

Patterns do not include seam allowances.
Add ¼" to patterns for appliqué
with turned-under edges.

Align this edge with top right piece of pattern B.

Align this edge with bottom piece of pattern B.

B (top left)

A

D

F

E

Align this edge with top left and right pieces of pattern B.

Patterns do not include seam allowances.
Add ¼" to patterns for appliqué
with turned-under edges.

B (bottom)

B (top right)

C

Align this edge with bottom piece of pattern B.

Align this edge with top left piece of pattern B.

SUMMERTIME SCATTER GARDEN

BLOOMING WITH BUTTONS AND BRIMMING WITH SUMMERTIME CHARM, THIS VIBRANT LITTLE QUILT CAN BE FASHIONED FROM SNIPPETS AND SCRAPS OF YOUR FAVORITE FABRICS IN NO TIME AT ALL. YOU'LL ENJOY YOUR VERY OWN COUNTRY GARDEN WITH EACH AND EVERY GLANCE.

Materials for Doll Quilt

⅜ yard *total* of assorted medium and dark print scraps for blocks and appliqués

¼ yard *total* of assorted light prints for blocks

1 fat quarter (18" x 22") of red stripe for border

1 fat eighth (9" x 22") of black print for border corner posts

Scraps of assorted green prints for stems

Enough 2½"-wide random lengths of assorted prints to make a 74" length of binding when joined end to end

⅝ yard of fabric for backing

21" x 24" piece of batting

⅜" bias bar

Liquid basting glue

22 small buttons in assorted neutral colors

Quilting thread in a neutral color

Cutting

Cut all strips across the width of the fabric unless otherwise noted. Refer to page 69 for appliqué patterns A–D and to "Invisible Machine Appliqué" on page 9 for pattern piece preparation.

From the assorted medium and dark print scraps, cut a *total* of:
160 squares, 1¼" x 1¼"
4 using pattern A
10 using pattern B
8 using pattern B reversed
4 using pattern C

From the assorted light prints, cut a *total* of:
48 squares, 2" x 2"

From the black print, cut:
4 squares, 3½" x 3½"

From the red stripe, cut:
2 rectangles, 3½" x 12½"
2 rectangles, 3½" x 9½"

From the assorted green print scraps, cut a *total* of:
2 strips, 1¼" x 9"
2 strips, 1¼" x 7½"

Piecing the X Blocks

1. Use a pencil to draw a diagonal line on the wrong side of 144 of the assorted medium and dark print 1¼" squares. Reserve the remaining 16 squares for later use.

2. With right sides together, layer a prepared 1¼" square over two opposite corners of an assorted light print 2" square. Stitch the layers exactly on the drawn lines. Press and trim the resulting triangles as instructed in "Pressing Triangle Units" on page 9. In the same manner, stitch, press, and trim a prepared square over a third corner. Repeat for a total of 48 pieced squares.

Make 48.

3. Lay out four pieced squares in two horizontal rows as shown to form an X block. Join the squares in each row. Press the seam allowances in opposite directions. Join the rows. Press the seam allowance to one side. Repeat for a total of twelve blocks measuring 3½" square.

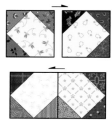

Make 12.

Assembling the Quilt Center

Lay out the blocks in four horizontal rows of three blocks each. Join the blocks in each row. Press the seam allowances of each row in opposite directions. Join the rows. Press the seam allowances in one direction. The pieced quilt center should now measure 9½" x 12½".

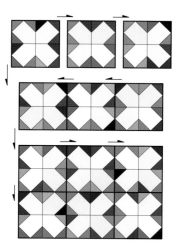

Designed, pieced, machine appliquéd, and hand quilted by Kim Diehl.

Finished quilt: 15½" x 18½" 🌼 **Finished block: 3" x 3"**

Piecing and Appliquéing the Borders

1. With right sides together, fold each black print 3½" square in half diagonally and lightly press the crease. Refold the square and lightly press a second diagonal crease.

2. Select a prepared A appliqué and center it on a black square by aligning the petal points with the creases. Baste in place. Referring to "Stitching the Appliqués" on page 12, stitch the appliqué.

Remove the paper pattern piece as instructed in "Removing Paper Pattern Pieces" on page 14. Repeat for a total of four appliquéd corner-post units.

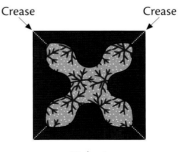

Make 4.

3. With right sides together, fold each red stripe rectangle in half lengthwise and lightly press the crease.

4. Join a creased red stripe 3½" x 12½" rectangle to the long sides of the quilt center. Press the seam allowances toward the red stripe. Join an appliquéd corner post to each end of the red stripe 3½" x 9½" rectangles. Carefully press the seam allowances away from the corner posts, taking care not to apply heat to the appliqués. Join these pieced border units to the remaining sides of the quilt center. Press the seam allowances toward the border units. The pieced quilt top should now measure 15½" x 18½".

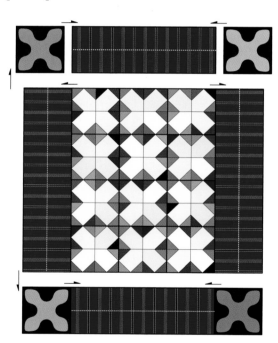

5. Referring to the quilt photo, lay out and baste the prepared B and B reversed appliqués along the border creases. (Position the first leaf on each border with the bottom tip resting on the corner-post seam line. Position the remaining leaves along the creases, placing them end to end where their straight edges meet.) Stitch the appliqués in place and remove the pattern pieces.

Note: For added flavor, the leaf appliqués on one border were reversed.

6. Using the assorted green 9"- and 7½"-long strips, prepare the stems as instructed in "Making Bias-Tube Stems and Vines" on page 12. Place tiny dots of liquid basting glue on the seam allowance of each 9" stem. Press one stem onto each long border, centering the stem over the leaf appliqués and overlapping one end approximately ⅛" onto the appliquéd corner-post flower. Using the 7½" stems, repeat this step on the remaining borders. Stitch the stems in place.

Overlap stem end approximately ⅛" onto flower appliqué.

Center each stem over leaf appliqués and pressed creases.

7. Select four reserved assorted print 1¼" squares and lay them out in two horizontal rows of two squares each to form a four-patch unit. Join the squares in each row. Press the seam allowances in opposite directions. Join the rows. Press the seam allowance to one side. Repeat for a total of four pieced four-patch units.

8. Trace and cut four D pattern pieces from freezer paper. Prepare one D appliqué from the center of each four-patch unit.

Note: The pattern pieces can easily be centered over the four-patch units by folding the paper in half twice and finger-pressing the creases. Align the pattern creases with the four-patch seams.

Make 4.

9. Referring to the quilt photo, stitch the C and D appliqués to the border. Remove the paper pattern pieces.

Completing the Quilt Top

Refer to "Finishing Techniques" on page 17 for details as needed. Layer the quilt top, batting, and backing. Quilt the layers. The featured quilt was hand quilted with intersecting diagonal lines over the X block centers and stitched in the ditch (over the seam lines) around the blocks. The borders were quilted along the lines of the stripes, and the appliqués were outlined for emphasis. Stitch the buttons to the quilt along the appliquéd stems, using a double strand of quilting thread and sliding the needle between the batting and fabric layers from button to button. Join the 2½"-wide random lengths of assorted medium and dark prints into one length and use it to bind the quilt.

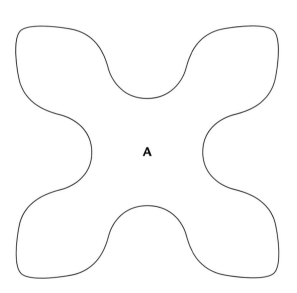

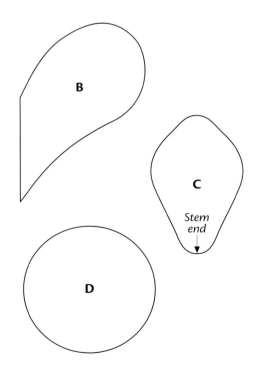

Patterns do not include seam allowances.
Add ¼" to patterns for appliqué
with turned-under edges.

SUMMER RECIPES

CONFETTI BEAN SALAD

This is one of my favorite summer salads. It can be served as a side dish at potlucks and barbeques, or even on its own with a cool drink when I'm in the mood for something light and quick.

1 can (16 ounces) kidney beans, drained but not rinsed
1 can (16 ounces) pinto beans, drained but not rinsed
1 can (16 ounces) black beans, drained but not rinsed
1 cup cucumber, peeled, seeded, and diced
½ cup diced red onion
1 celery stalk, halved lengthwise and then sliced
¼ cup ranch dressing
½ teaspoon garlic powder
⅛ to ¼ teaspoon ground cayenne pepper, optional
Salt and pepper
2 to 3 Roma tomatoes, seeded and diced
1½ cups thinly sliced fresh spinach

Combine the beans, cucumber, onion, celery, ranch dressing, garlic powder, and cayenne pepper in a large serving bowl; season with salt and pepper to taste. Cover and refrigerate for 1 to 2 hours or until well chilled. Just before serving, gently stir in the tomatoes and spinach.

DILLED PASTA SALAD

I often make this delicious salad in the morning or even the night before I plan to serve it, because it becomes even more flavorful as it chills. It's perfect paired with grilled meat on a hot summer day.

1½ cups penne pasta, uncooked
1½ cups chopped fresh broccoli
1 cup peeled, seeded, and diced cucumber
¾ cup diced red onion
1 cup diced cheddar cheese

Dressing

½ cup mayonnaise
½ cup light sour cream
¼ cup milk
1 teaspoon dried dill weed
½ teaspoon salt
Freshly ground pepper

Cook the pasta in salted water according to the package instructions. Rinse with cold water; drain well. Place the pasta in a large serving bowl with the broccoli, cucumber, onion, and cheese. Whisk together the dressing ingredients. Pour over the pasta mixture and toss gently to coat. Chill at least 1 hour before serving. If the pasta absorbs the dressing, stir in a splash of milk before serving.

SUMMERTIME GRILLING MARINADE

Pour this yummy marinade over your favorite meat in the afternoon and let the flavors work their
magic until you grill that evening. This mixture is especially good with pork chops and chicken breasts.

1 cup teriyaki sauce
2 tablespoons packed brown sugar
1 teaspoon garlic powder
3 green onions, sliced, white and some green parts

Whisk together the marinade ingredients. Pour over the meat of your choice in a glass bowl
or a resealable plastic bag. Refrigerate several hours, turning the meat occasionally. Remove the
meat from the marinade and grill to the desired doneness. Discard the remaining marinade.

QUICK CHERRY CRISP

A buttery, homemade crust and crumbly oat topping are the perfect finish to store–bought
cherry pie filling in this pretty dessert.

Pastry

1 cup flour
½ cup packed brown sugar
⅛ teaspoon salt
¼ pound (1 stick) cold butter

Filling

1 can (20 ounces) cherry pie filling
1 can (14 ounces) cherry pie filling

Topping

1⅔ cups quick-cooking rolled oats
¼ cup flour
½ cup packed brown sugar
6 tablespoons butter, melted

Preheat the oven to 350°. In a mixing bowl,
combine the first three pastry ingredients.
Cut in the butter until crumbled to the size of
peas. Press the pastry mixture into the bottom
of a 9 x 13-inch baking dish and bake for 15
minutes. Pour both cans of cherry pie filling
onto the baked crust. Combine all of the
topping ingredients and sprinkle over the filling.
Continue baking for 20 to 25 minutes, or until
the top is golden brown and bubbly around the
edges. Serve warm with a scoop of vanilla ice
cream.

DUCK, DUCK, GOOSE

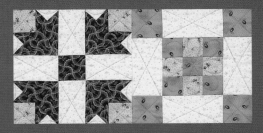

FILLED WITH THE COLORS OF FALLING LEAVES AS THEY DANCE THROUGH YOUR BLOSSOMING MUMS, THIS PATCHWORK LAP QUILT INVITES YOU TO WRAP YOURSELF IN WARMTH AND COMFORT AS YOU CURL UP IN YOUR FAVORITE ARMCHAIR AND WATCH THE SEASONS CHANGE.

Materials for Lap Quilt

⅙ yard *each* of 29 assorted prints in fall hues for blocks and outer border

2 yards of light tan print for block backgrounds and inner border

¾ yard of green print for blocks, outer border, and binding

⅝ yard of medium tan print for block backgrounds

3¾ yards of fabric for backing

67" x 76" piece of batting

Cutting

Cut all strips across the width of the fabric unless otherwise noted.

From the light tan print, cut:

3 strips, 3" x 42"; crosscut into 30 squares, 3" x 3". Cut each square in half diagonally once to yield 60 triangles.

12 strips, 2½" x 42"; reserving 6 strips, crosscut 6 strips into 60 rectangles, 2½" x 4"

8 strips, 2¾" x 42"; crosscut into 60 rectangles, 2¾" x 5"

From the medium tan print, cut:

4 strips, 2¼" x 42"; crosscut into 60 squares, 2¼" x 2¼"

3 strips, 2" x 42"; crosscut into 60 squares, 2" x 2"

For the Goose Tracks blocks, from *each* of 14 assorted prints *and* the green print, cut:

2 squares, 3" x 3"; cut each square in half diagonally once to yield 4 triangles (60 total)

2 squares, 4⅜" x 4⅜"; cut each square in half diagonally once to yield 4 triangles (60 total)

1 square, 2½" x 2½" (15 total)

For the Framed Nine Patch blocks, from *each* of the remaining 15 assorted prints, cut:

5 squares, 2" x 2" (75 total)

4 squares, 2¾" x 2¾" (60 total)

From the remainder of the green print, cut:

7 strips, 2½" x 42" (binding)

From the remainder of the green print and assorted prints, cut a *total* of:*

90 rectangles, 2½" x 6½"

49 squares, 2½" x 2½"

80 squares, 1½" x 1½"

6 rectangles, 2½" x 4½"

4 rectangles, 2½" x 3½"

For added flavor, a handful of rectangles and squares in the featured quilt were cut from look-alike scraps.

Piecing the Goose Tracks Blocks

1. Select one matching set of assorted print patchwork pieces cut for the Goose Tracks blocks. With right sides together, layer an assorted print and light tan print 3" triangle. Sew along the long bias edges. Press the seam allowance toward the assorted print. Trim away the dog-ear points. Repeat for a total of four half-square-triangle units.

Make 4.

2. Cut each half-square-triangle unit in half diagonally once as shown to yield eight pieced triangles.

Make 8.

3. Join the dark side of a pieced triangle to one side of a medium tan 2¼" square. Press the seam allowance toward the tan print. Join the dark side of a second pieced triangle to the adjacent side of the square. Press the seam allowance toward the tan print. Trim away the dog-ear points. Repeat for a total of four pieced triangle units.

Make 4.

4. Sew each triangle unit to a matching print 4⅜" triangle to make four corner units. Press the seam allowances toward the whole triangle. Trim away the dog-ear points.

Make 4.

Designed and pieced by Kim Diehl. Machine quilted by Celeste Freiberg.

Finished quilt: 61½" x 70½" ✿ Finished block: 9" x 9"

5. Lay out four corner units, four light tan print 2½" x 4" rectangles, and one matching print 2½" square in three horizontal rows to form a block. Join the pieces in each row. Press the seam allowances toward the tan print. Join the rows. Press the seam allowances toward the middle row.

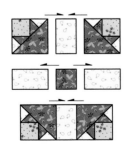
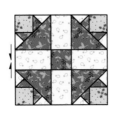

6. Repeat steps 1–5 for a total of 15 Goose Tracks blocks measuring 9½" square.

Piecing the Framed Nine Patch Blocks

1. Select one matching set of assorted print patchwork pieces cut for the Framed Nine Patch blocks. Lay out five assorted print 2" squares and four medium tan print 2" squares in three horizontal rows to form a nine-patch unit. Join the squares in each row. Press the seam allowances toward the assorted prints. Join the rows. Press the seam allowances away from the middle row.

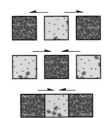

2. Join a light tan 2¾" x 5" rectangle to opposite sides of the nine-patch unit. Press the seam allowances toward the tan print.

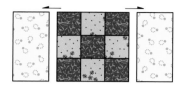

3. Sew a matching assorted print 2¾" square to the ends of a light tan print 2¾" x 5" rectangle. Press the seam allowances toward the tan print. Repeat for a total of two pieced rectangles. Join these rectangles to the remaining edges of the nine-patch unit. Press the seam allowances away from the nine-patch unit.

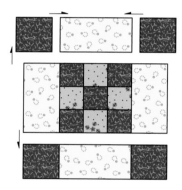

4. Repeat steps 1–3 for a total of 15 Framed Nine Patch blocks measuring 9½" square.

Assembling the Quilt Center

Lay out the Goose Tracks blocks and Framed Nine Patch blocks in six horizontal rows, as shown, alternating the block positions from row to row. Join the blocks in each row. Press the seam allowances toward the Framed Nine Patch blocks. Join the rows. Press the seam allowances toward the rows that

begin with a Framed Nine Patch block. The pieced quilt center should now measure 45½" x 54½".

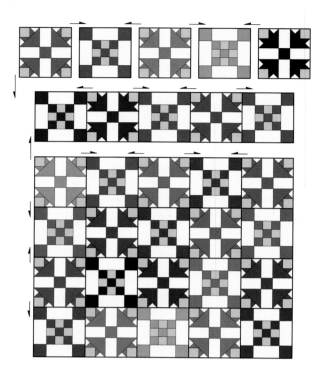

Adding the Borders

1. For the inner border, join the six reserved light tan print 2½" x 42" strips end to end. Press the seam allowances to one side. From this pieced strip, cut two strips that are 54½" long for the side borders and two strips that are 49½" long for the top and bottom borders. Join the side borders to the right and left sides of the quilt center. Press the seam allowances away from the quilt center. Join the top and bottom borders to the remaining sides of the quilt center. Press the seam allowances away from the quilt center.

2. For the pieced outer border, select six assorted print 1½" squares and join them end to end. Press the seam allowances in one direction. Repeat for a total of 12 small checkerboard units.

Make 12.

3. Select three assorted print 2½" squares and join them end to end. Press the seam allowances in one direction. Repeat for a total of 15 large checkerboard units.

Make 15.

4. Referring to the quilt photo for placement, lay out 23 assorted print 2½" x 6½" rectangles, four small checkerboard units, and four large checkerboard units for the left side border. Or, simply arrange the pieces in a way that is pleasing to you. Join the pieces. Press the seam allowances in one direction. Join this border to the left side of the quilt top. Press the seam allowances toward the quilt center.

5. Repeat step 4 using 23 assorted print 2½" x 6½" rectangles, two small checkerboard units, and five large checkerboard units to make and attach the right side border.

6. Repeat step 4 *twice* using 20 assorted print 2½" x 6½" rectangles, three small checkerboard units, and three large checkerboard units for the top and bottom borders.

7. Join and press four assorted print 1½" squares, two assorted print 2½" x 3½" rectangles, one assorted print 2½" x 4½" rectangle, and one assorted print 2½" x 6½" rectangle as shown to form corner-post unit A. Repeat for a total of two A units.

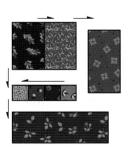
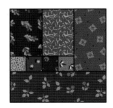

Corner-post unit A.
Make 2.

8. Join and press two assorted print 2½" squares, two assorted print 2½" x 4½" rectangles, and one assorted print 2½" x 6½" rectangle as shown to form corner-post unit B. Repeat for a total of two B units.

Corner-post unit B.
Make 2.

9. Referring to the quilt photo, join a corner-post A and B unit to one end of the top and bottom border rows. Press the seam allowances toward the corner posts. Sew these borders to the remaining sides of the quilt top. Press the seam allowances toward the quilt center. The pieced quilt top should now measure 61½" x 70½".

Completing the Quilt

Refer to "Finishing Techniques" on page 17 for details as needed. Layer the quilt top, batting, and backing. Quilt the layers. The featured quilt was machine quilted with Xs stitched onto the background rectangles and squares of the blocks, the dark center square of the Goose Tracks blocks, and the dark outer squares of the Framed Nine Patch blocks. A teardrop medallion was stitched onto the center of each Nine Patch block. Free-form figure-eights were quilted onto the assorted print foregrounds of the corner units of the Goose Tracks blocks, radiating from the inner point outward. A running chain and diamond design was quilted onto the inner border, and Xs were stitched onto the rectangles and squares of the outer border. Join the seven green print 2½" x 42" strips into one length and use it to bind the quilt.

THINGS THAT GRIN IN THE NIGHT

AUTUMN-HUED PRINTS AND PLAIDS COMBINE WITH BIG, TOOTHY GRINS FOR A WHIMSICAL LITTLE WALL HANGING THAT'S ANYTHING BUT SPOOKY. SO CHARMING AND LOVABLE, THESE COLORFUL CHARACTERS WILL MAKE YOU WISH EVERY DAY WERE HALLOWEEN!

Materials for Wall Quilt

4½" x 24" rectangle *each* of 6 assorted cream prints for fence

⅜ yard of small-scale medium blue check or print for sky

⅜ yard *total* of 2 different tan prints for border

⅜ yard *total* of assorted dark print scraps for border

⅛ yard of purple print for grass

1 fat quarter (18" x 22") *each* of 2 different orange prints or plaids for large and medium pumpkins

1 fat eighth (9" x 22") of orange print or plaid for small pumpkin

1 fat quarter of black print for cat

6" x 6" square of gold print for moon

Scraps of assorted prints, including browns and greens, for appliqués

Scraps of muslin for eye and teeth appliqués

⅜ yard of black print for binding

1 yard of fabric for backing

34" x 42" piece of batting

Scraps of batting for stuffed appliqué embellishments

Fabric glue stick

Liquid basting glue

⅜" bias bar

Water-soluble marker

#8 black perle cotton

Size 5 embroidery needle

8 assorted dark buttons for eyes, in matching pairs

Cutting

Cut all strips across the width of the fabric unless otherwise noted. Refer to pages 83–91 for the appliqué patterns and to "Invisible Machine Appliqué" on page 9 for pattern piece preparation. For greater ease, cutting specifications for the appliqués are provided as they are used.

From the blue check or print, cut:
1 rectangle, 10¼" x 24½"

From the purple print, cut:
1 rectangle, 3" x 24½"

From the assorted print scraps for the border, cut a _total_ of:
28 rectangles, 2½" x 4½"
4 squares, 2½" x 2½"

From the 2 different tan prints, cut a _total_ of:
56 squares, 2½" x 2½"

From the black print for binding, cut:
4 strips, 2½" x 42"

Making the Fence Unit

1. Join the six assorted cream print 4½" x 24½" rectangles along the long edges, stopping and backstitching 1¼" from the top edge of each seam. Press the seam allowances open.

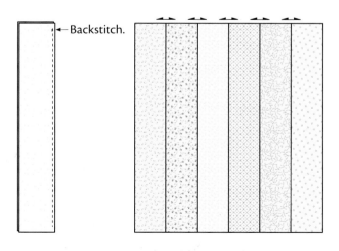

Backstitch.

2. Referring to "Invisible Machine Appliqué" and using the pattern on page 90, cut six fence-top pattern pieces from freezer paper. Use a small amount of glue from the fabric glue stick on the nonwaxy side of a prepared pattern piece and anchor it to the wrong side of one fence rectangle, about ¼" from the top raw edge. Trim away the excess fabric at each corner, leaving a ¼" seam allowance. Press the seam allowance onto the waxy side of the pattern piece to form the top of the fence board. Repeat with the remaining fence rectangles.

Appliquéing the Sky Unit

1. Using the patterns on pages 83 and 84 and referring to the materials list on page 79 for the fabrics needed, prepare the cat and moon appliqués. (The number of pieces needed for each appliqué shape is indicated on the patterns.)

2. Referring to the quilt photo, lay out the cat and moon appliqués on the blue print 10¼" x 24½" rectangle, positioning the straight edges of the cat body and tail so they are flush with the rectangle bottom edge. Position the cat paws at an angle, with the point of the inner raw edge resting on the rectangle bottom edge. When you're happy with the placement, trim away the excess bottom portion of each paw.

Note: To simplify the placement and stitching of the mouth appliqué for the moon, fold the end of the prepared shape under on the dashed line and position it on the moon with the folded edge tucked underneath; anchor it with a pin. After basting the moon onto the background, fold the top portion of the mouth back and pin it to the background. As the moon is stitched, the mouth will be anchored to the background at the fold. After removing the paper pattern piece from the moon, reposition and stitch the top portion of the mouth for stitching.

Designed, pieced, machine appliquéd, and hand quilted in the big-stitch method by Kim Diehl.

Finished quilt: 28½" x 36½"

3. Referring to "Stitching the Appliqués" on page 12, work from the bottom layer to the top to stitch the shapes in place, remembering to remove the paper pattern pieces between each layer as instructed in "Removing Paper Pattern Pieces" on page 14.

Assembling the Quilt Center

1. Referring to the quilt photo, lay the pieced fence unit onto the appliquéd sky unit, overlapping the fence so that the bottom edge of the sky unit rests about ½" below the inner "V" shapes; pin or baste. (Drops of liquid basting glue under the pressed seam allowance of the fence will simplify this process.) Appliqué the fence to the sky unit along the top fence line. Working on the wrong side, trim away the excess sky fabric inside the fence line, leaving a generous ¼" seam allowance. Remove the paper pattern pieces from the fence unit.

2. Measuring down from the top edge of the sky rectangle, use an acrylic ruler and rotary cutter to trim the bottom edge of the fence unit so the height of the fence and sky units combined is 30½".

3. Join the purple print 3" x 24½" rectangle to the bottom edge of the fence unit. Press the seam allowance away from the fence.

Stitching the Pumpkin Appliqués

1. From the scraps of one green print, cut enough 1½"-wide bias lengths to equal a 24"-long strip when joined end to end using straight, not diagonal, seams. Referring to "Making Bias-Tube Vines and Stems" on page 12, prepare the vine.

2. Using the patterns on pages 85–91 and referring to the materials list on page 79 for the fabrics needed, prepare the remaining appliqués and work from the bottom layer to the top to lay out and stitch them in place. Remember to remove the paper pattern pieces before adding each new layer.

   Note: When working with the large and medium pumpkins, take extra care to baste the appliqués securely to prevent them from shifting.

3. Measuring from the top of the sky unit, trim any excess grass to bring the total measurement of the quilt center to 32½" long and 24½" wide.

Piecing and Adding the Border

1. Use a pencil to draw a diagonal line on the wrong side of each tan print 2½" square.

2. With right sides together, layer a prepared tan square over one end of an assorted print 2½" x 4½" rectangle. Stitch, press, and trim as instructed in "Pressing Triangle Units" on page 9. In the same manner, join a second prepared tan print square to the remaining end of the rectangle as shown. Repeat for a total of 28 flying-geese units.

Make 28.

3. Join eight flying geese units end to end to make a border strip. Press the seam allowances to one side. Repeat for a total of two border strips.

Make 2.

4. Join the border strips from step 3 to the right and left sides of the quilt center with the tan triangles on the outside edge. Carefully press the seam allowances toward the quilt center, taking care not to apply heat to the appliqués.

5. Repeat step 3 to make two border strips of six flying-geese units each. Sew an assorted print 2½" square to each end of these pieced strips. Press the seam allowances toward the squares. Join these strips to the remaining sides of the quilt center. Carefully press the seam allowances toward the quilt center. The pieced quilt top should now measure 28½" x 36½".

Stuffing the Appliqués

Referring to "Stuffed Appliqués" on page 16, stuff any appliqués you wish to accent. On the featured quilt, the eye and teeth appliqués were stuffed.

Completing the Quilt

Referring to the quilt photo, use a water-soluble marker to draw tooth lines onto each mouth appliqué. Referring to "Stem Stitch" on page 16, use the size 5 embroidery needle and perle cotton to stitch the teeth lines. Layer the quilt top, batting, and backing. Quilt the layers. The featured quilt was hand quilted in the big-stitch method, with free-form wood grain lines sewn onto the fence. Each appliqué was outlined for emphasis, and the sky area was echo quilted around the shapes. Free-form "cinnamon roll" circles were stitched onto the grass area, and the border patchwork was outlined ¼" to each side of the seam lines. Sew buttons onto the eyes of each pumpkin, cat, and moon appliqué, sliding the needle and thread under the batting to prevent shadowing. Join the five black print 2½" x 42" strips into one length and use it to bind the quilt.

Cat head
Make 1.

Cat eye
Make 2.

Cat nose
Make 1.

Cat lips
Make 1.

Patterns do not include
seam allowances.
Add ¼" to patterns
for appliqué with
turned-under edges.

Cat body
Make 1.

Cat teeth
Make 1.

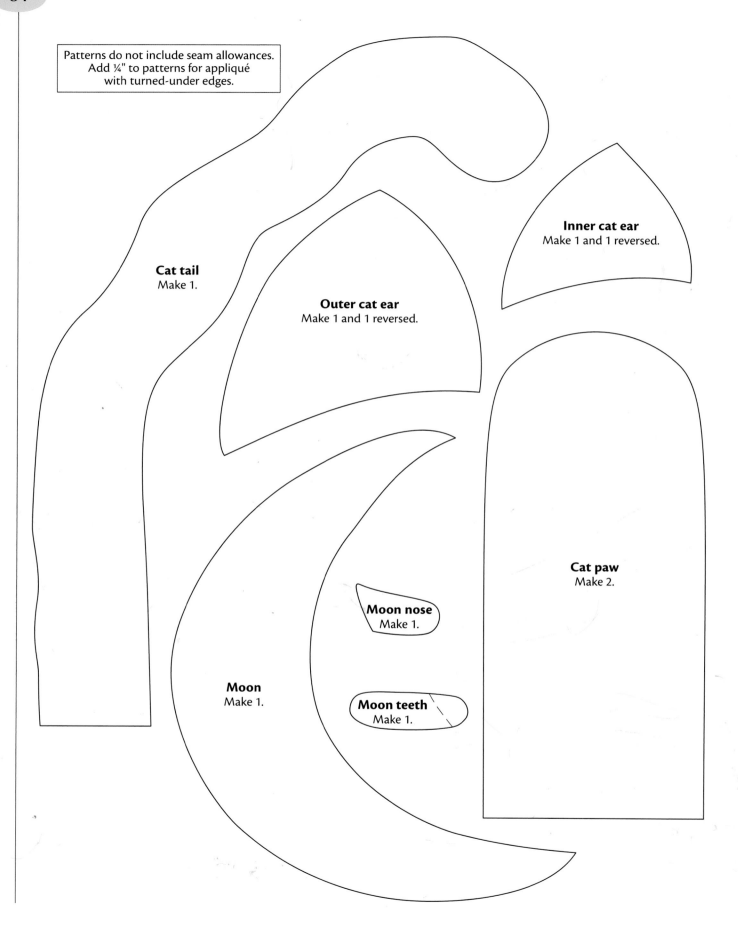

Patterns do not include seam allowances.
Add ¼" to patterns for appliqué
with turned-under edges.

Cat tail
Make 1.

Outer cat ear
Make 1 and 1 reversed.

Inner cat ear
Make 1 and 1 reversed.

Cat paw
Make 2.

Moon nose
Make 1.

Moon
Make 1.

Moon teeth
Make 1.

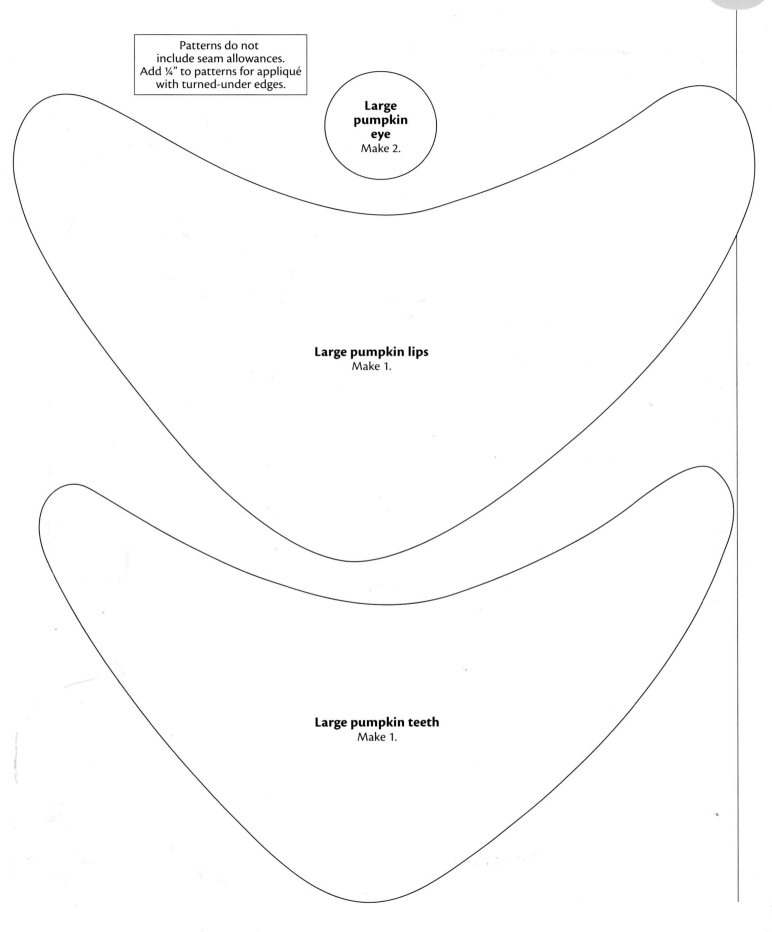

Patterns do not
include seam allowances.
Add ¼" to patterns for appliqué
with turned-under edges.

**Large
pumpkin
eye**
Make 2.

Large pumpkin lips
Make 1.

Large pumpkin teeth
Make 1.

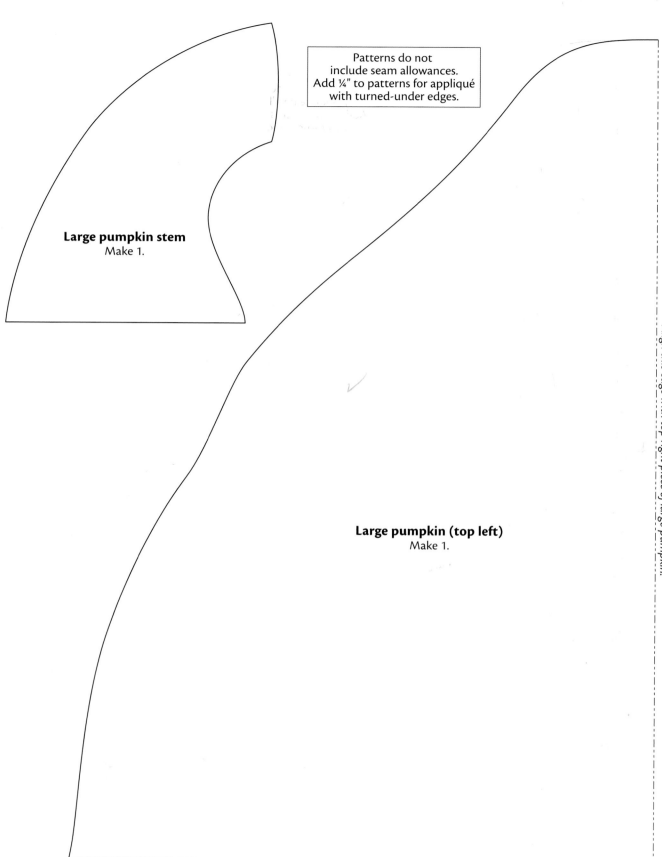

Patterns do not
include seam allowances.
Add ¼" to patterns for appliqué
with turned-under edges.

Large pumpkin stem
Make 1.

Large pumpkin (top left)
Make 1.

Align this edge with top right piece of large pumpkin.

Align this edge with bottom piece of large pumpkin.

Patterns do not
include seam allowances.
Add ¼" to patterns for appliqué
with turned-under edges.

Large pumpkin nose
Make 1.

Align this edge with top left piece of large pumpkin.

Large pumpkin (top right)
Make 1.

Align this edge with bottom piece of large pumpkin.

Align this edge with top left piece of large pumpkin.

Large pumpkin (bottom)
Make 1.

Place this edge on fold of freezer paper measuring 10" x 20" that has been folded in half to make a square. Cut shape on solid line and unfold pattern.

Pattern does not
include seam allowance.
Add ¼" to pattern for appliqué
with turned-under edge.

AUTUMN PENNIES

REMINISCENT OF A WOOL PENNY RUG, THESE BRILLIANT BULL'S-EYE CIRCLES AND TRIANGLE PATCHES ARE SOFTENED WITH RAVEN BLACK BORDERS AND HAND-SEWN STITCHES FOR A TABLETOP QUILT THAT'S STUNNING IN ITS SIMPLICITY.

Materials for Tabletop Quilt

1½ yard *total* of assorted print scraps (5" squares and smaller) for Penny block appliqués

¾ yard of black print for border

⅞ yard of tan print for Penny block backgrounds

1¼ yards *total* of assorted medium and dark prints for Quarter-Square-Triangle blocks and binding

2⅞ yards of fabric for backing

51" x 51" square of batting

Cutting

Cut all strips across the width of the fabric unless otherwise noted. Refer to page 95 for appliqué patterns A–D and to "Invisible Machine Appliqué" on page 9 for pattern piece preparation.

From the assorted medium and dark prints, cut a *total* of:

24 squares, 6¼" x 6¼"; cut each square in half diagonally once to yield 48 triangles

Enough 2½"–wide random lengths to make a 192" length of binding when joined end to end

From the tan print, cut:

29 squares, 5½" x 5½"

From the assorted print scraps, 5" and smaller, cut a *total* of:

29 using pattern A

29 using pattern B

29 using pattern C

29 using pattern D

From the black print, cut:

4 strips, 5½" x 35½"

Piecing the Quarter-Square-Triangle Blocks

1. With right sides together, join two assorted print triangles along the long bias edges. Press the seam allowance to one side. Trim away the dog-ear points. Repeat for a total of 24 half-square-triangle units.

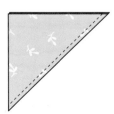 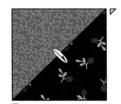

Make 24.

2. Cut each half-square-triangle unit in half diagonally as shown to yield 48 pieced triangles.

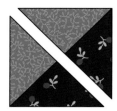

3. Select two pieced triangles sewn from different prints. Repeat step 1 to join the pieced triangles. Repeat for a total of 24 Quarter-Square-Triangle blocks measuring 5½" square.

Make 24.

Appliquéing the Penny Blocks

1. With right sides together, fold each tan print 5½" square in half vertically and lightly press the crease. Refold horizontally and lightly press a second crease.

2. Select a prepared A, B, C, and D appliqué. Carefully fold and finger-press vertical and horizontal creases in each.

3. Beginning with the A appliqué, align the finger-pressed creases with the creases on the background square; baste the appliqué to the background. Referring to "Stitching the Appliqués" on page 12, stitch the appliqué in place. Remove the pattern piece as instructed in "Removing Paper Pattern Pieces" on page 14.

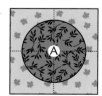

Align creases.

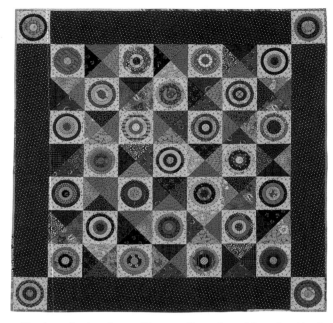

Designed, pieced, machine appliquéd, and hand quilted in the big-stitch method by Kim Diehl.

Finished quilt: 45½" x 45½"
Finished block: 5" x 5"

4. In the same manner, work from the bottom layer to the top to stitch the B, C, and D appliqués. Remember to remove the paper pattern pieces before adding each new layer.

5. Repeat steps 2–4 for a total of 29 Penny blocks measuring 5½" square.

Assembling the Quilt Center

Lay out the Penny blocks and Quarter-Square-Triangle blocks in seven horizontal rows of seven blocks each, alternating the position of the blocks from row to row. Reserve the remaining four Penny blocks for later use. Join the blocks in each row. Carefully press the seam allowances toward the

Penny blocks, taking care not to apply heat to the appliqués. Join the rows. Press the seam allowances in one direction. The pieced quilt center should now measure 35½" square.

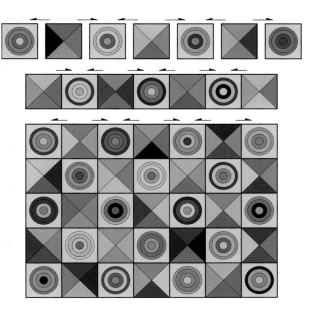

Adding the Border

1. Join a black print 5½" x 35½" strip to the right and left sides of the quilt center. Carefully press the seam allowances toward the borders.

2. Sew a reserved Penny block to the ends of the remaining black print 5½" x 35½" strips. Carefully press the seam allowances toward the black print. Join these pieced strips to the remaining sides of the quilt center. Press the seam allowances toward the borders. The finished quilt top should now measure 45½" square.

Make 2.

Completing the Quilt

Refer to "Finishing Techniques" on page 17 for details as needed. Layer the quilt top, batting, and backing. Quilt the layers. The featured quilt was hand quilted in the big-stitch method, with the penny shapes outlined for emphasis. The penny appliqué patterns were used as quilting guides to stitch circles over the Quarter-Square-Triangle blocks and onto the borders. One larger circle was quilted around each set of penny shapes, including the appliqué blocks, to allow the outer circles to intersect and fill in the background areas. Join the 2½"-wide random lengths of assorted medium and dark prints into one length and use it to bind the quilt.

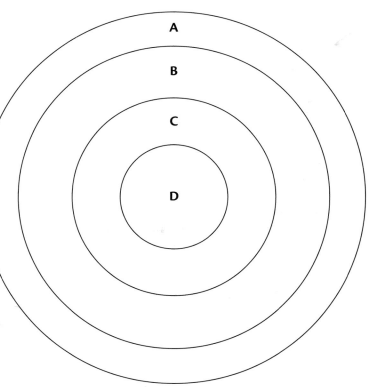

Patterns do not include seam allowances.
Add ¼" to patterns for appliqué with turned-under edges.

TAFFY PULL

THANKFUL THOUGHTS, A GRATEFUL
SPIRIT, AND THE BOUNTY OF NATURE'S
HARVEST ARE PERFECT COMPLEMENTS
TO THIS SIMPLY PIECED QUILT CERTAIN
TO BRING A TOUCH OF QUAINT,
UNDERSTATED WARMTH AND CHARM
TO ANY ROOM.

Materials for Bed Quilt

6½ yards *total* of assorted medium and dark print scraps
    for blocks and border
½ yard *each* (or equivalent scraps) of 5 assorted tan
    prints for blocks and sashing
1½ yards of red print for blocks, border, and binding
6 yards of fabric for backing
80" x 98" piece of batting

Cutting

From the assorted tan prints, cut a *total* of:

Cut all strips across the width of the fabric unless otherwise noted.

96 squares, 1½" x 1½"

96 rectangles, 1½" x 3½"

96 rectangles, 1½" x 5½"

96 rectangles, 1½" x 7½"

24 rectangles, 1½" x 9½"

4 rectangles, 1½" x 10½"

From the red print, cut:

344 squares, 1½" x 1½"

9 strips, 2½" x 42" (binding)

From 1 assorted medium or dark print, cut the following pieces for 1 set:

1 rectangle, 1½" x 3½"

1 rectangle, 1½" x 5½"

1 rectangle, 1½" x 7½"

1 rectangle, 1½" x 9½"

Repeat to cut a total of 96 sets. Keep the pieces from each set together.

From the remainder of the medium and dark prints, cut a *total* of:

296 rectangles, 1½" x 4½"

148 rectangles, 1½" x 5½"

148 rectangles, 1½" x 3½"

Piecing the Courthouse Steps Blocks

Due to the numerous seams this block contains, I suggest using a slightly scant ¼" seam allowance to achieve a finished block of accurate size. Refer to the block assembly diagram below as you piece each block.

1. Join an assorted tan print 1½" square to opposite sides of a red print 1½" square. Press the seam allowances toward the red print.

2. Select two different sets of assorted medium or dark prints. Sew the 1½" x 3½" rectangles, one from each print, to the remaining sides (long sides) of the step 1 unit. Press the seam allowances toward the new rectangles.

3. Join an assorted tan print 1½" x 3½" rectangle to each seamed side of the unit from step 2. Press the seam allowances toward the tan print. Continue adding rectangles in numerical order as shown, matching the medium or dark prints on the top and bottom portions of the block and pressing the seam allowances toward each new rectangle.

Block assembly

4. Repeat steps 1–3 for a total of 48 Courthouse Steps blocks measuring 9½" square.

Designed by Kim Diehl. Pieced by Barbara Walsh, Kim Williams, and Kim Diehl.
Machine quilted by Celeste Freiberg.

Finished quilt: 74½" x 92½" ❀ **Finished block:** 9" x 9"

Assembling the Quilt Center

Lay out the blocks in eight horizontal rows of six blocks each. Join the blocks in each row. Press the seam allowances of each row in opposite directions. Join the rows. Press the seam allowances in one direction.

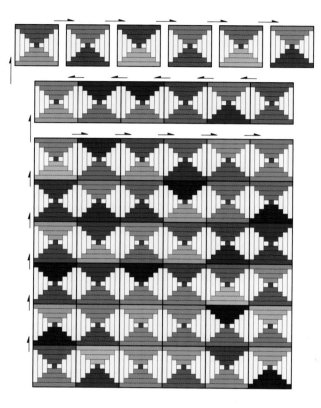

Piecing and Adding the Borders

1. To make the inner pieced border, join eight assorted tan print 1½" x 9½" rectangles end to end. Press the seam allowances in one direction. Repeat for a total of two pieced border strips. Join these pieced strips to the right and left sides of the quilt center, matching the border seams with the block row seams. Press the seam allowances toward the border strips.

2. Sew four assorted tan 1½" x 9½" rectangles together end to end. Add an assorted tan print 1½" x 10½" rectangle to each end of the strip. Press the seam allowances in one direction. Repeat for a total of two pieced border strips. Join these strips to the remaining sides of the quilt center, matching the seams as before. Press the seam allowances toward the border strips. The pieced quilt top should now measure 56½" x 74½".

3. To make the outer pieced border, join two assorted medium or dark print 1½" x 4½" rectangles to the sides of a red print 1½" square. Press the seam allowances toward the red print. Repeat for a total of 148 A units.

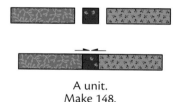

A unit.
Make 148.

4. Join an assorted medium or dark print 1½" x 5½" rectangle and an assorted medium or dark print 1½" x 3½" rectangle to the sides of a red print 1½" square. Press the seam allowances toward the red print. Repeat for a total of 148 B units.

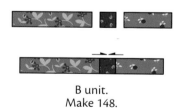

B unit.
Make 148.

5. Lay out 37 A units and 37 B units in alternating positions as shown. Join the units to form a border row. Press the seam allowances in one direction. Repeat for a total of four outer border rows.

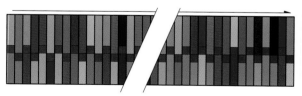

Make 4.

6. Sew an outer border to the right and left sides of the quilt top. Press the seam allowances toward the quilt center. Sew the remaining borders to the remaining sides of the quilt top. Press the seam allowances toward the quilt center. The pieced quilt top should measure 74½" x 92½".

Completing the Quilt

Refer to "Finishing Techniques" on page 17 for details as needed. Layer the quilt top, batting, and backing. Quilt the layers. The featured quilt was machine quilted with a swirling design as described on page 19. The borders were stitched with a serpentine feathered vine wrapping around the perimeter and small feathered branches extending from the main vine to fill the open areas. Join the nine red 2½" x 42" strips into one length and use it to bind the quilt.

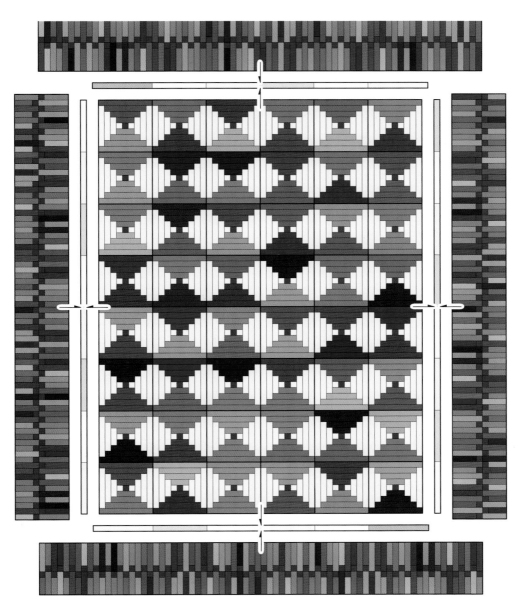

AUTUMN RECIPES

FARMHOUSE ROLLS

So quick and easy to make, these are my favorite rolls when I'm in the mood to bake. They're the perfect accompaniment to soups and salads, and as they bake, your home will be filled with the most inviting aroma!

4 to 5 cups all-purpose flour
2 packages rapid-rise yeast
1 teaspoon salt
4 tablespoons sugar
4 tablespoons (½ stick) butter
1½ cups milk

In a large mixing bowl (I use a stand mixer with a bread hook attachment), combine 4 cups of the flour with the yeast, salt, and sugar. Heat the butter and milk to 125° to 130° and add it to the flour mixture, mixing for approximately 1 minute. Add as much of the remaining flour as needed, ¼ cup at a time, until a very soft dough forms. Knead for 2 minutes or until the dough is smooth and elastic. Place the dough into an oiled bowl, cover with plastic wrap, and set it in a warm place for approximately 15 minutes.

Punch the dough down and divide it in half, taking out one half and leaving the other in the bowl. Cover the bowl to keep the dough from drying out. Divide the remaining dough into 12 equal pieces and roll each into a smooth, golf ball-size piece. Place the balls in a lightly greased 9"-round cake pan. Repeat with the remaining half of the dough. Cover the pans with a towel and allow the dough to rise in a warm place for 20 to 30 minutes. Bake at 375° for 10 to 15 minutes, until very lightly browned.

Makes 24 dinner rolls.

HEARTY SPLIT PEA SOUP

Once the crisp days of autumn arrive, there are few things I love more than the smell of soup simmering on the stove. This flavorful and filling recipe is one of my husband's favorites.

1 package (16-ounces) split peas
8 cups chicken broth
1 medium onion, diced
6 strips of thick-sliced bacon
1 ham steak, cut into large dices
1 can (14½ ounces) sliced carrots, cut into fourths
½ teaspoon dried thyme

Place the peas and chicken broth in a large stock pan; bring to a boil over medium heat. Skim any foam with a slotted spoon. Reduce the heat, cover, and simmer for 1 hour. Add the onions. Cover and continue simmering for another hour. Meanwhile, slice the bacon crosswise into 1" pieces and fry until crisp. Drain the bacon, reserving about 1 tablespoon of fat. Stir the soup until smooth. Add the bacon and bacon fat, ham, carrots, and thyme, and simmer an additional 30 minutes.

SPICED PUMPKIN BREAD

So incredibly moist and full of spicy fall flavors, this bread is what my daughters ask for most as the weather cools and the leaves begin to blush with color. The icing also makes a wonderful dip for fresh fruit during the summer months and is especially good served with a plate of whole strawberries.

Bread

3½ cups flour
3 cups sugar
2 teaspoons baking soda
1 teaspoon salt
1 teaspoon ground cinnamon
1 teaspoon ground ginger
½ teaspoon ground cloves
¼ teaspoon ground nutmeg
4 eggs
1 cup vegetable oil
⅔ cup water
2 cups canned pumpkin

Icing

1 package (8 ounces) light cream cheese, softened
1 tablespoon butter, softened
½ teaspoon vanilla
1¼ cups powdered sugar

In a large mixing bowl, stir together the flour, sugar, baking soda, salt, and spices. Combine the eggs, oil, water, and pumpkin, and mix into the dry ingredients until blended. Pour into five greased and floured mini loaf pans. Bake at 350° for 30 to 40 minutes, or until a toothpick inserted in the middle of the loaf comes out clean. Remove the loaves from the pans; cool to room temperature. Place the loaves in resealable plastic bags or wrap with plastic wrap and store in the refrigerator. As they chill, the loaves will become very moist.

Blend the icing ingredients until smooth and serve with the sliced loaves.

FROST ON THE WINDOWPANE

SETTLE IN BY THE HEARTH AND CHASE THE FROST AWAY WITH THIS COZY QUILT FASHIONED FROM BURNISHED SHADES OF CRANBERRY AND OLIVE GREEN. SPICY MULLED CIDER, STRINGS OF FRESH CRANBERRIES, AND YOUR FAVORITE WINTER SOCKS ARE ALL YOU'LL NEED FOR A FEELING OF OLD-FASHIONED GOODNESS.

Materials for Lap Quilt

2⅞ yards of cream print for block background

1⅞ yards *total* of assorted olive green prints for blocks

1¾ yards *total* of assorted cranberry prints for blocks and binding

4 yards of fabric for backing

70" x 70" square of batting

Cutting

Cut all strips across the width of the fabric unless otherwise noted.

From the cream print, cut:
20 strips, 4½" x 42"; crosscut into 160 squares, 4½" x 4½"

From the assorted cranberry prints, cut a *total* of:
256 squares, 1½" x 1½"
36 squares, 4½" x 4½"
Enough 2½"-wide random lengths to form a 266" length of binding when joined end to end

From the assorted olive green prints, cut a *total* of:
384 squares, 1½" x 1½"
60 squares, 4½" x 4½"

Piecing and Assembling the Quilt Center

1. Use a pencil to draw a diagonal line on the wrong side of the cranberry print 1½" squares.

2. With right sides together, layer a prepared cranberry print 1½" square over opposite corners of a cream print 4½" square. Stitch the layers exactly on the drawn lines. Press and trim the resulting triangles as instructed in "Pressing Triangle Units" on page 9. Repeat on the remaining corners. Repeat for a total of 64 pieced blocks measuring 4½" square.

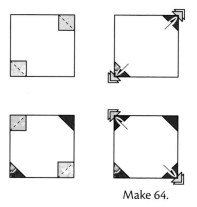

Make 64.

3. Lay out the blocks in eight horizontal rows of eight blocks each. Join the blocks in each row. Press the seam allowances of each row in opposite directions. Join the rows. Press the seam allowances in one direction. The pieced quilt center should now measure 32½" square.

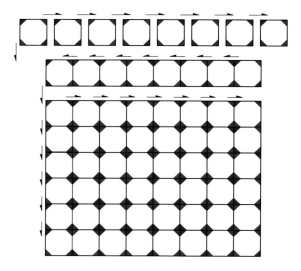

Assembling and Adding the First Border

1. Join eight assorted cranberry print 4½" squares end to end to make a border strip. Press the seam allowances in one direction. Repeat for a total of two border strips. Join these strips to the right and left sides of the quilt center. Press the seam allowances away from the quilt center.

Designed by Kim Diehl. Pieced and machine quilted by Delene Kohler.

Finished quilt: 64½" x 64½" ❀ **Finished block:** 4" x 4"

2. Join ten assorted cranberry print 4½" squares as instructed in step 1. Repeat for a total of two border strips. Join these strips to the remaining sides of the quilt center. Press the seam allowances away from the quilt center.

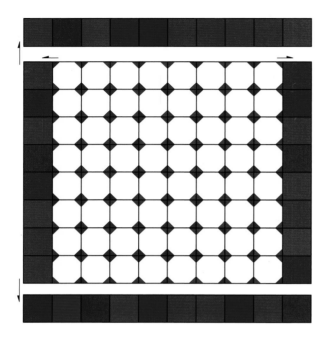

Piecing and Adding the Second Border

1. Use a pencil to draw a diagonal line on the wrong side of the olive print 1½" squares.

2. Referring to step 2 of "Piecing and Assembling the Quilt Center" on page 106, make a total of 96 blocks measuring 4½" square.

3. Lay out 20 blocks in two horizontal rows of ten blocks each. Join the blocks in each row. Press the seam allowances of each row in alternating directions. Join the rows to make a border unit. Press the seam allowances to one side. Repeat for a total of two border units. Join these border units to the right and left sides of the quilt top. Press the seam allowances toward the quilt center.

4. Referring to step 3, lay out and piece 28 blocks in two horizontal rows of 14 blocks each. Repeat for a total of two border units. Join these units to the remaining sides of the quilt top. Press the seam allowances toward the quilt center.

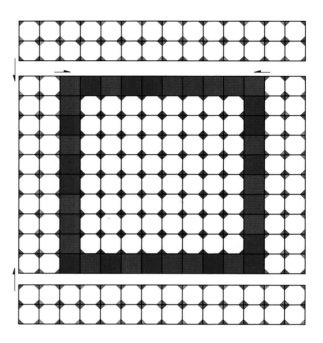

Piecing and Adding the Third Border

1. Join 14 assorted olive print 4½" squares as instructed in step 1 of "Assembling and Adding the First Border" on page 106. Repeat for a total of two pieced border strips. Join these strips to the right and left sides of the quilt top. Press the seam allowances away from the quilt center.

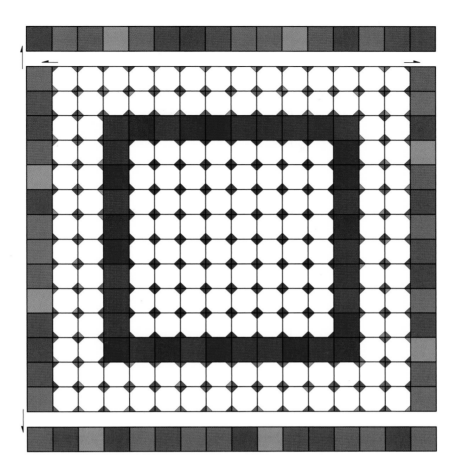

2. In the same manner, join 16 assorted olive print 4½" squares. Repeat for a total of two pieced border strips. Join these strips to the remaining sides of the quilt top. Press the seam allowances away from the quilt center. The pieced quilt top should now measure 64½" square.

Completing the Quilt Top

Refer to "Finishing Techniques" on page 17 for details as needed. Layer the quilt top, batting, and backing. Quilt the layers. The featured quilt was machine quilted with a snowflake design centered on the cream print background portion of each pieced block and a small stipple filling in the remaining background areas. The cranberry and olive green borders were quilted with a simplified snowflake pattern on the seam between each block, with an X stitched onto each square. A scalloped line was stitched along the outer portion of each X to create a stylized swag. Join the 2½"-wide random lengths of assorted cranberry prints into one length and use it to bind the quilt.

CHRISTMAS MAGIC

REMEMBER CHILDHOOD HOLIDAYS WITH BOUGHS OF EVERGREENS AND SPRIGS OF MISTLETOE, EARNEST LETTERS TO SANTA, AND COOKIES ON A PLATE BY THE TWINKLING TREE? RECAPTURE THESE MOMENTS AS YOU STITCH THIS LITTLE QUILT BURSTING WITH THE MAGIC OF CHRISTMAS.

Materials for Tabletop Quilt

2½ yards of tan print for blocks and borders

1 fat quarter (18" x 22") *each* of 3 assorted red prints for blocks and outer border

1 fat quarter *each* of 2 assorted green prints for blocks and outer border

1 fat quarter *each* of 2 assorted brown prints for block, outer border, and branch appliqués

1 fat quarter of gold print for block, star appliqués, and outer border

1 fat quarter of blue print for block and outer border

1 fat quarter of cream print for snowman appliqués

1 fat quarter of green plaid for holly leaf appliqués

1 fat quarter of red stripe for outer pomegranate appliqués

1 fat eighth (9" x 22") of contrasting red print for inner pomegranate appliqués

1 fat eighth of red print for bow appliqués

Scraps of light and dark blue prints for hat appliqués

Scraps of orange print for carrot nose appliqués

½ yard of green stripe for binding

3 yards of fabric for backing

54" x 54" square of batting

³⁄₁₆" bias bar

Water-soluble marker

20 black buttons in assorted sizes for snowmen

40 red buttons in assorted sizes for berries

#8 black perle cotton

Size 5 embroidery needle

Cutting

Cut all strips across the width of the fabric unless otherwise noted. Refer to page 117 for appliqué patterns A–J and to "Invisible Machine Appliqué" on page 9 for pattern piece preparation.

From the *lengthwise grain* of the tan print, cut:
2 strips, 9½" x 42½"
2 strips, 9½" x 24½"
2 squares, 6½" x 6½"

From the remainder of the tan print, cut:
1 strip, 6½" x 42"; crosscut into 6 squares, 6½" x 6½"
20 strips, 1½" x 42"; crosscut into:
  • 184 rectangles, 1½" x 2½"
  • 176 squares, 1½" x 1½"
4 squares, 1⅞" x 1⅞"; cut each square in half diagonally once to yield 8 triangles

From *each* of the 8 fat quarters for blocks, cut:
44 squares, 1½" x 1½" (352 total)
11 squares, 2½" x 2½" (88 total)

From the remainder of one green fat quarter, cut:
8 squares, 1½" x 1½"
2 squares, 2⅞" x 2⅞"; cut each square in half diagonally once to yield 4 triangles

From the cream print, cut:
4 using pattern A

From the brown fat quarter for the branches, cut:
8 strips, 1" x 18"
16 rectangles, 1" x 2¼"
8 rectangles, 1" x 1½"

From the scraps of dark blue print, cut:
4 using pattern B

From the scraps of light blue print, cut:
4 using pattern C

From the red print for the bows, cut:
4 using pattern D
4 using pattern E

From the scraps of orange print, cut:
4 using pattern F

From the green plaid, cut:
20 using pattern G*
For added flavor, a handful of the G appliqués were cut from the remainder of the green fat quarters used for the blocks.

From the red stripe, cut:
24 using pattern H

From the contrasting red print, cut:
24 using pattern I

From the remainder of the gold print fat quarter, cut:
16 using pattern J

From the green stripe, cut:
5 strips, 2½" x 42" (binding)

Piecing the Blocks

1. Use a pencil to draw a diagonal line on the wrong side of 88 tan print 1½" squares.

2. Using the red, green, gold, blue, and brown print squares, select a matching set of four 1½" squares and one 2½" square. Use a pencil to draw a diagonal line on the wrong side of the 1½" squares.

3. With right sides together, layer a prepared red, green, gold, blue, or brown print 1½" square over one end of a tan print 1½" x 2½" rectangle as shown. Stitch the pair exactly on the drawn line. Press and trim as instructed in "Pressing Triangle Units" on page 9. Layer a second prepared square of the same color over the remaining end of the rectangle as shown. Stitch, press, and trim as previously instructed. Repeat for a total of two pieced rectangles.

Make 2.

Designed, pieced, and machine appliquéd by Kim Diehl. Machine quilted by Celeste Freiberg.

Finished quilt: 48½" x 48½" ☘ **Finished block:** 6" x 6"

4. Join a pieced rectangle to one side of a matching print 2½" square. Press the seam allowance away from the pieced rectangle. Join a tan print 1½" square to one end of the remaining pieced rectangle as shown. Press the seam allowance toward the tan print. Join this pieced unit to the adjacent side of the 2½" square. Press the seam allowance toward the 2½" square.

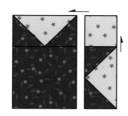

5. Layer a prepared tan print 1½" square over a unit from step 4. Stitch, press, and trim as previously instructed.

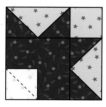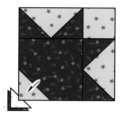

6. Repeat steps 2–5 for a total of 88 pieced block units.

7. Select four matching block units. Lay out the units in two horizontal rows to form a block. Join the units in each row. Press the seam allowances in alternating directions. Join the rows. Press the seam allowance to one side. Repeat for a total of three red print blocks, two green print blocks, and one each of blue, gold, and brown print blocks. Each block should measure 6½" square. Reserve the remaining block units for later use.

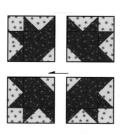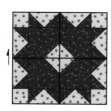

Make 8 total.

Assembling the Quilt Center

Lay out eight blocks and eight tan print 6½" squares in four horizontal rows as shown. Join the pieces in each row. Press the seam allowances toward the tan squares. Join the rows. Press the seam allowances in one direction. The pieced quilt center should now measure 24½" square.

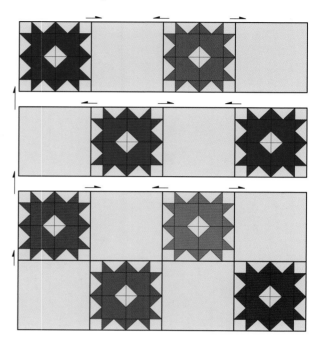

Adding and Appliquéing the Middle Border

1. Join a tan print 9½" x 24½" strip to the right and left sides of the quilt center. Press the seam allowances toward the tan strip. Join a tan print 9½" x 42½" strip to the remaining sides of the quilt center. Press the seam allowances toward the tan strip.

2. Lightly press a diagonal crease at each border corner, extending from the corner of the quilt center to the outer point of the middle border. Carefully fold a prepared A appliqué in half

vertically and finger-press a crease. Line up the crease of the snowman with the background crease, positioning it about 1¾" from each border edge; baste in place. Repeat with the remaining corners.

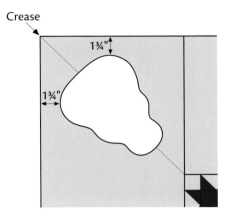

Crease

1¾"

1¾"

3. Referring to "Stitching the Appliqués" on page 12, stitch each snowman. Remove the paper pattern pieces as instructed in "Removing Paper Pattern Pieces" on page 14.

4. Referring to "Making Bias-Tube Stems and Vines" on page 12, use a scant ¼" seam allowance to stitch and prepare the brown print strips and rectangles cut for the branches. Using the quilt photo as a guide, lay out one prepared 18" length, two 2¼" lengths, and one 1½" length on each side of the snowmen. (The branch pieces have been cut on the straight of grain, so they will be a bit gnarly and knobby when laid out, rather than smooth and flowing.) After ensuring that the raw ends of the short stems are tucked securely under the main branches, baste and stitch the appliqués. Repeat with the remaining corners of the quilt top.

5. Referring to the quilt photo, work from the bottom layer to the top to lay out and stitch the remaining appliqués to the quilt top, remembering to remove the paper pattern pieces before adding each new layer.

   Note: If you find it difficult to prepare the small nose appliqués, use fusible web, following the

manufacturer's instructions. Fuse the pieces to the snowmen and satin stitch the raw edges with matching thread.

Piecing and Adding the Outer Border

1. Select 14 reserved block units sewn from an assortment of prints. Join the units end to end to form a pieced border strip. Press the seam allowances in one direction. Repeat for a total of four pieced border strips.

Make 4.

2. Join a pieced border strip to the right and left sides of the quilt top. Carefully press the seam allowances toward the middle border, taking care not to apply heat to the appliqués.

3. Join a tan print 1⅞" triangle to one side of a green print 1½" square. Press the seam allowance toward the tan print. In the same manner, sew and press a second tan triangle to the adjacent side of the green square. Trim away the dog-ear points. Join this pieced triangle to a green print 2⅞" triangle as shown. Press the seam allowance toward the green print. Repeat for a total of four pieced square units.

Make 4.

4. Join a tan print 1½" x 2½" rectangle to a pieced square unit from step 3 as shown on page 116. Press the seam allowance toward the rectangle. Join a green print 1½" square to one end of a tan

print 1½" x 2½" rectangle. Press the seam allowance toward the tan print. Join this pieced rectangle to the adjacent side of the pieced square. Press the seam allowance toward the pieced rectangle. Repeat for a total of four Corner Post blocks.

Make 4.

5. Referring to the quilt photo, join a Corner Post block to the ends of the remaining pieced border strips. Press the seam allowances toward the Corner Post blocks. Join these border strips to the remaining sides of the quilt top. Carefully press the seam allowances toward the middle border. The pieced quilt top should now measure 48½" square.

Completing the Quilt

Refer to "Finishing Techniques" on page 17 for details as needed. Layer the quilt top, batting, and backing. Quilt the layers. The featured quilt was machine quilted with a feathered wreath stitched around the tan center of each block and tiny holly leaves stitched at the block points. This design repeats in the setting squares and the outer border blocks. The background areas of the quilt were filled in with McTavishing (free-form outlines that are echo quilted inward). The snowmen were textured with gently waving lines interspersed with tiny snowflakes.

Use a water-soluble marker to draw dots on each snowman face as a guide for sewing the French knots at the mouth and eyes. Referring to "French Knots" on page 16, use the size 5 embroidery needle and perle cotton to stitch the faces, sliding the needle under the batting between each knot to prevent shadowing. Use the perle cotton to sew five black buttons in assorted sizes to each snowman body, again sliding the needle under the batting layer. Stitch five assorted red buttons to each branch, taking care to cover the raw stem ends and hide the thread lines underneath the batting.

Join the five green striped 2½" x 42" strips into one length and use it to bind the quilt.

Patterns do not
include seam allowances.
Add ¼" to patterns for appliqué
with turned-under edges.

C

B

I

F

A

H

D

G

J

E

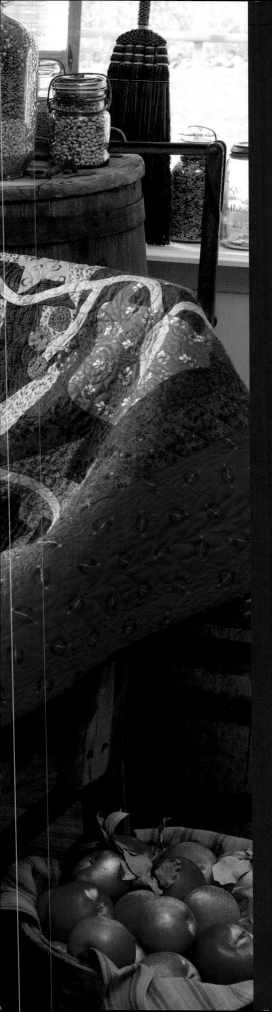

WINTERBERRIES

ENJOY BLUSTERY, SNOW-SWEPT DAYS
ENSCONCED IN THE SOFTNESS OF THIS RICHLY
HUED QUILT.
TRADITIONAL
PATCHWORK BLOCKS,
BASKETS OF TRAILING
BERRY-LADEN VINES,
AND A TWINKLING
OF STARS WILL
HELP CHASE THE
CHILL AWAY AS YOU
ANTICIPATE THE
WARM AND SUNNY
DAYS OF SPRING.

Materials for Lap Quilt

⅙ yard *each* of 12 assorted prints for Churn Dash blocks

⅙ yard *each* of 12 contrasting prints for Churn Dash block
   backgrounds

1¼ yards of cranberry print for outer border

⅝ yard of dark green print for inner border

10½" x 10½" square *each* of 4 assorted prints for Basket
   block backgrounds

1 fat eighth (9" x 22") *each* of 4 assorted dark tan or gold
   prints for basket appliqués

1 fat eighth *each* of 3 assorted green prints for leaf appliqués

1 fat quarter (18" x 22") of light green print for vine
   appliqués and inner border corner posts

Scraps of red and assorted prints for berry and star
   appliqués

⅝ yard of black print for binding

3¾ yards of fabric for backing

65" x 65" square of batting

½" bias bar

Cutting

Cut all strips across the width of the fabric unless otherwise noted. Refer to page 125 for appliqué patterns A–E and to "Invisible Machine Appliqué" on page 9 for pattern piece preparation.

From *each* of the 12 assorted prints for the Churn Dash blocks, cut pieces for 1 set:

2 squares, 4⅞" x 4⅞"; cut each square in half
 diagonally once to yield 4 triangles (48 total)
1 strip, 2½" x 14" (12 total)

From *each* of the 12 contrasting prints for the Churn Dash block backgrounds, cut pieces for 1 set:

2 squares, 4⅞" x 4⅞"; cut each square in half
 diagonally once to yield 4 triangles (48 total)
1 strip, 2½" x 14" (12 total)
1 square, 2½" x 2½" (12 total)

From *each* of the dark tan or gold print fat eighths, cut:

1 using pattern A (4 total)
1 using pattern B (4 total)

From the *straight grain* of the light green print fat quarter, cut:

Enough 1½"-wide lengths to equal a 170" length
 when joined end to end

From the remainder of the light green print fat quarter, cut:

6 strips, 1½" x 5"
2 rectangles, 1½" x 2"
4 squares, 2½" x 2½"

From the 3 assorted green prints, cut a *total* of:

13 using pattern C

From the assorted print scraps, cut a *total* of:

8 using pattern D

From the assorted red print scraps, cut a *total* of:

49 using pattern E

From the dark green print, cut:

6 strips, 2½" x 42"; crosscut into:
 • 4 strips, 2½" x 40½"
 • 8 rectangles, 2½" x 7½"

From the cranberry print, cut:

5 strips, 7½" x 42"; crosscut into:
 • 4 strips, 7½" x 40½"
 • 4 squares, 7½" x 7½"

From the black print, cut:

6 strips, 2½" x 42" (binding)

Piecing the Churn Dash Blocks

1. Select a matching set of patchwork pieces cut for a Churn Dash block and a contrasting set of pieces cut for the block background. From these pieces, join two assorted print 2½" x 14" strips (one from each set) along the long edges to make a strip set. Press the seam allowance away from the print designated for the background. Crosscut the strip set into four segments, 2½" wide.

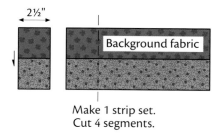

2½"

Background fabric

Make 1 strip set.
Cut 4 segments.

2. Join two 4⅞" triangles (one from each set) along the long bias edges. Press the seam allowances away from the print designated for the background. Trim away the dog-ear points. Repeat for a total of four half-square-triangle units.

Make 4.

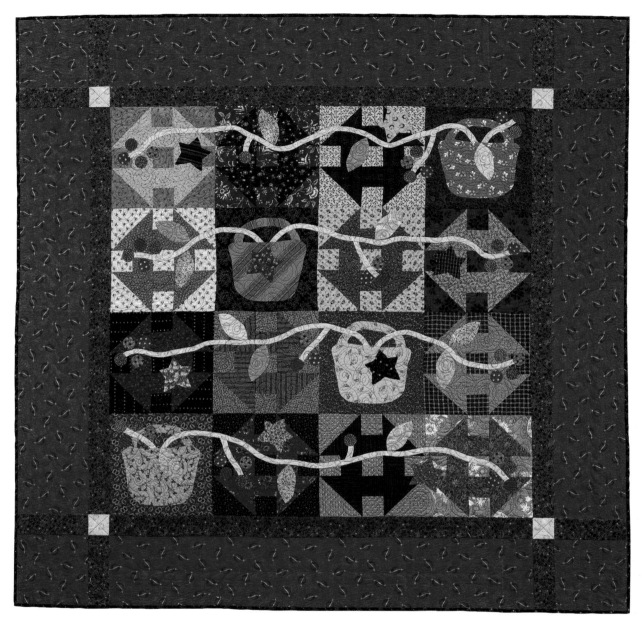

Designed, pieced, and machine appliquéd by Kim Diehl.
Machine quilted by Celeste Freiberg and Kathy Ockerman.

Finished quilt: 58½" x 58½" ❀ **Finished block:** 10" x 10"

3. Lay out four half-square-triangle units, four segments from step 1, and one background print 2½" square in three horizontal rows to form a Churn Dash block. Join the pieces in each row. Press the seam allowances toward the strip-set segments. Join the rows. Press the seam allowances toward the middle row.

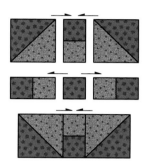
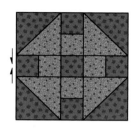

4. Repeat steps 1–3 for a total of 12 Churn Dash blocks measuring 10½" square.

Appliquéing the Basket Blocks

1. With right sides together, fold an assorted print 10½" square in half vertically and lightly press the crease. Select a prepared matching print A and B appliqué. Carefully fold the A appliqué in half vertically and finger-press the fold at the top and bottom edges.

2. Align the basket crease with the crease of the block background, placing the basket approximately 1¼" from the bottom raw edge. Position the B appliqué on the background above the basket, tucking the raw handle edges under the basket approximately ¼"; baste the handle in place. Remove the basket. Referring to "Stitching the Appliqués" on page 12, stitch the handle. Remove the paper pattern piece as instructed in "Removing Paper Pattern Pieces" on page 14. Reposition and appliqué the basket, leaving an

unstitched 2"- to 3"-wide area at the top center edge to add the vines. Remove the paper pattern piece.

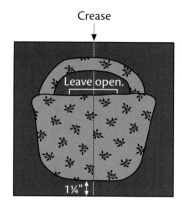

3. Repeat steps 1 and 2 for a total of four appliquéd Basket blocks measuring 10½" square.

Assembling and Appliquéing the Quilt Center

1. Lay out the blocks in four horizontal rows of three Churn Dash blocks and one Basket block each as shown. Join the blocks. Carefully press the seam allowances of each row in alternating directions, taking care not to apply heat to the appliqués.

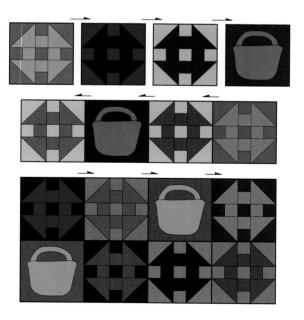

2. Join the light green print 1½"-wide vine strips end to end using straight seams. Referring to "Making Bias-Tube Stems and Vines" on page 12, prepare the 170" vine, the 5" stem lengths, and the 2" stem lengths. From the prepared vine, cut two pieces 38" long, two pieces 28" long, and two pieces 17" long.

3. Referring to the quilt photo (or altering the placement to please yourself), lay out and stitch the appliqués for each row, working from the bottom layer to the top, as follows:

> **Row 1:** One 38" vine, two 5" stems, and one 2" stem, ensuring the raw ends of the stems are tucked under the vine approximately ¼". After the vines and stems are stitched, add three leaf appliqués, two star appliqués, and 12 berry appliqués.
>
> **Row 2**: One 28" vine, one 17" vine, and one 5" stem. Add three leaf appliqués, two star appliqués, and 12 berry appliqués.
>
> **Row 3**: One 28" vine, one 17" vine, and one 5" stem. Add 4 leaf appliqués, two star appliqués, and 12 berry appliqués.
>
> **Row 4**: One 38" vine, two 5" stems, and one 2" stem. Add 3 leaf appliqués, two star appliqués, and 13 berry appliqués.

4. Appliqué the openings at the top of each basket where the vines were inserted and ensure that all paper pattern pieces have been removed.

5. Lay out rows 1–4 in numerical order, working from the top to the bottom. Join the rows. Carefully press the seam allowances in one direction, taking care not to apply heat to the

appliqués. The pieced quilt center should now measure 40½" square.

Piecing and Adding the Borders

1. Join a dark green print 2½" x 40½" strip to the right and left sides of the quilt center. Press the seam allowances toward the green strips.

2. Join a medium-light green print 2½" square to each end of the remaining 2½" x 40½" strips. Press the seam allowances toward the strips. Join these pieced strips to the remaining sides of the quilt center. Press the seam allowances toward the dark green strips.

3. Join a dark green print 2½" x 7½" rectangle to each end of two cranberry print 7½" x 40½" strips. Press the seam allowances toward the cranberry print. Join these strips to the right and left sides of the quilt top. Press the seam allowances toward the inner border.

Make 2.

4. Join a dark green print 2½" x 7½" rectangle to each end of the remaining two cranberry print 7½" x 40½" strips. Press the seam allowances toward the green print. Add a cranberry print 7½" square to the ends of these strips. Press the seam allowances toward the squares. Join these pieced strips to the remaining sides of the quilt top. Press the seam allowances toward the inner border. The pieced quilt top should measure 58½" square.

Make 2.

Completing the Quilt

Refer to "Finishing Techniques" on page 17 for details as needed. Layer the quilt top, batting, and backing. Quilt the layers. The center of the featured quilt was machine quilted with a swirling design as described on page 19, and Xs were stitched onto the dark green inner border and corner-post units to form cross-hatching. A feathered vine was quilted along the middle of each cranberry print outer border strip, with a feathered X placed onto each cranberry print corner-post square. A small stipple design was used to fill the space behind the feathered motifs. Join the six black print 2½" x 42" strips into one length and use it to bind the quilt.

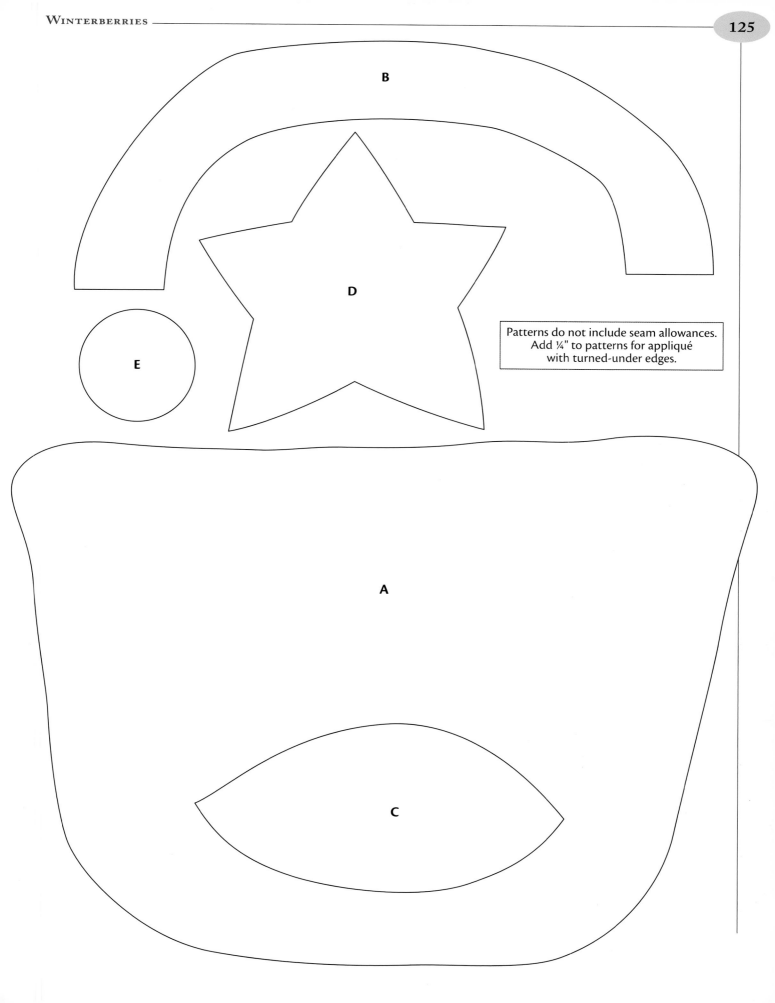

B

D

E

Patterns do not include seam allowances.
Add ¼" to patterns for appliqué
with turned-under edges.

A

C

WINTER RECIPES

PARTY APPETIZERS

*One recipe, two yummy appetizers! Make these for your next
holiday party or football celebration and watch them disappear.*

1 puff pastry sheet

8 slices bacon

1 pound medium whole mushrooms, cleaned

2 packages (8 ounces) light cream cheese, softened

4 green onions, finely chopped, white and some green parts

1 egg, lightly beaten

1 teaspoon garlic powder

½ teaspoon salt

Grated Parmesan cheese, paprika, and dried parsley flakes for garnish

Thaw the puff pastry according to the package instructions. Meanwhile, in a skillet, cook and crumble the
bacon; drain the fat, leaving just enough to cover the skillet bottom. Place half of the mushrooms in a food
processor. Remove the stems from the remaining mushrooms and add to the food processor, reserving the
caps. Pulse the mushrooms until finely chopped. Sauté the chopped mushrooms in the skillet over medium-
high heat until the moisture evaporates and they're tender, about 5 minutes. In a large mixing bowl, blend the
sautéed mushrooms, bacon, cream cheese, green onions, egg, garlic powder, and salt. Cover and refrigerate 1 to
2 hours until firm.

Lightly coat three mini muffin pans and one foil-lined cookie sheet with nonstick cooking spray. Cut the
pastry sheet lengthwise into six rows, and each row into six pieces. Place a pastry piece into the bottom of
each prepared muffin cup and use a measuring teaspoon or melon baller to place a scoop of filling onto each.
Sprinkle each appetizer with a pinch of Parmesan, parsley, and paprika (or, for a little zip, ground cayenne
pepper). Place the reserved mushroom caps open side up onto the prepared cookie sheet; season with salt and
pepper to taste. Fill and garnish the caps as instructed for the pastries. Bake at 375° for 15 to 20 minutes or
until lightly browned. Serve warm.

COUNTRY POTATO CHOWDER

So flavorful and hearty, a steaming bowl of this chowder is the perfect way to fill you up and keep you toasty warm on a chilly day.

3 medium *or* 2 large baking potatoes
1 pound sliced bacon, cut into 1" pieces
3 cups fresh mushrooms, sliced
8 cups milk (½ gallon total), divided
¼ cup chicken bullion granules
⅓ cup all-purpose flour
½ teaspoon garlic powder
½ teaspoon celery salt
3 green onions, sliced, white and some green parts
2 cans (15 ounces) whole kernel corn, drained
1 teaspoon dried parsley flakes

Cut the potatoes in half and boil them in their jackets in salted water until tender. Drain and let rest until cool enough to handle; peel and cut into large dice. Meanwhile, in a heavy stock pot, cook the bacon until crisp. Transfer the bacon to a paper towel; drain the fat, leaving just enough to cover the bottom of the pot. Add the mushrooms and sauté over medium-high heat until tender, about 5 minutes. Reduce the heat to medium and add 7 cups of the milk.

Place the bullion granules and flour into a small mixing bowl and whisk in 1 cup of milk. Stir into the stock-pot mixture. Add the garlic powder, celery salt, and green onions. When the milk mixture is very warm and begins to thicken slightly, stir in the potatoes, corn, and bacon; season with salt and pepper to taste. Reduce the heat to low. Warm slowly until ready to serve, at least 30 minutes, without simmering. Stir in the parsley flakes just before serving.

RASPBERRY TRUFFLES

What could be better at Christmastime than rich and decadent chocolates with a delicate hint of raspberry and a dusting of lightly sweetened cocoa? A chocolate-lover's dream!

¼ pound (1 stick) salted butter
½ cup heavy whipping cream
2 packages (12 ounces) semisweet chocolate chips
¼ cup plus 1 tablespoon seedless raspberry jam
⅓ cup cocoa powder
⅓ cup powdered sugar

Bring the butter and whipping cream just to a simmer over medium heat in a heavy saucepan. Reduce the heat, add the chocolate chips, and whisk until smooth. Remove from the heat and stir in the raspberry jam. Pour the mixture into a bowl and freeze 1 hour or until firm enough to mold. Form into 1" balls and set on wax paper-lined cookie sheets. Refrigerate until set, about 1 hour. Meanwhile, gently sift the cocoa powder and powdered sugar into a small bowl. Roll the truffles briefly between your palms to smooth them, and then roll them in the cocoa mixture. Makes 40 to 50 truffles.

ABOUT THE AUTHOR

After chancing upon a sampler quilt pattern at a sidewalk sale in 1997, Kim Diehl set about to make her first quilt without the benefit of any quiltmaking knowledge or experience and soon discovered she had found a new passion.

With just her third quilt, Kim entered and won *American Patchwork & Quilting* magazine's "Pieces of the Past" quilt challenge in 1998. This win took her life down a new and unexpected path, and Kim began designing quilts professionally soon after. In the years since, Kim has seen many of her designs published in national magazines, and she remains a frequent contributor to *American Patchwork & Quilting*. When she's not designing and sewing patchwork, Kim enjoys traveling to guilds and events around the country, sharing her quilts and teaching her invisible machine appliqué methods.

Simple Seasons, Kim's third book with Martingale & Company, is near and dear to her heart because it brings together her love of traditional patchwork and appliqué with her passion for cooking and creating recipes.

Kim makes her home in scenic Idaho surrounded by her family, her much-spoiled pooches, and her country-style gardens.

Acknowledgments

To Delene Kohler, Deslynn Mecham, Kathy Ockerman, Pat Peyton, Barbara Walsh, and Kim Williams, thanks so much for our shared love of quilting, your beautiful workmanship, and your generous spirits.

To Celeste Freiberg, thank-you for your exquisite machine quilting that truly is the icing on the cake as I make my quilts.

A big hug for my daughters, Katie and Molly, and my almost daughter, Sara Peyton, for your help while we photographed the quilts and taste-tested some of my pinch-of-this and dash-of-that recipes.

For my friend Michelle Price, thank-you for your gracious hospitality and your willingness to share your wonderful home a second time as we photographed several of the quilts among your beautiful treasures.

To the staff of Martingale & Company, I'd like to express my appreciation for your creative abilities and skills that enable me to produce books I can be proud of. My special thanks to Stan Green and Brent Kane for your insight and patience during the photo shoot, as I draped quilts and lace over anything that didn't move.

To Janome America, many thanks for the use of your Memory Craft 11000 sewing machine. With each new project, I love it even more!

My sincere thanks to Fairfield Processing Corporation for your Soft Touch batting, which helps produce the soft and comfy quilts my family loves to wrap up in.